Wit

D0678151

9|26|13
$15.99
B&T
As

REPLY ALL...
And Other
Ways to Tank
Your Career

REPLY ALL...

And Other Ways to Tank Your Career

RICHIE FRIEMAN

St. Martin's Griffin
New York

REPLY ALL . . . AND OTHER WAYS TO TANK YOUR CAREER. Copyright © 2013 by Richie Frieman. All rights reserved. Printed in the United States of America. For information, address St. Martin's Press, 175 Fifth Avenue, New York, N.Y. 10010.

www.stmartins.com

Design by Michelle McMillian

Library of Congress Cataloging-in-Publication Data

Frieman, Richie.
   Reply all-and other ways to tank your career / Richie Frieman.
      pages cm
   ISBN 978-1-250-03726-8 (trade paperback)
   ISBN 978-1-4668-4314-1 (e-book)
   1. Business etiquette.   2. Self-presentation.   3. Interpersonal relations.   I. Title.
   HF5389.F75 2013
   395.5'2—dc23   2013013845

St. Martin's Griffin books may be purchased for educational, business, or promotional use. For information on bulk purchases, please contact Macmillan Corporate and Premium Sales Department at 1-800-221-7945, extension 5442, or write specialmarkets@macmillan.com.

First Edition: September 2013

10 9 8 7 6 5 4 3 2 1

To my beautiful wife,
JAMIE,
I'm so lucky.

To my awesome kids,
MADDY *and* COLE,
you have no idea how amazing
you have made my life.
Please remember this when you're teenagers
and trying to avoid me like the plague.

Contents

REPLY ALL . . .
And Other
Ways to Tank
Your Career

Introduction

Allow me to paint a picture of my first year out of college (or as every cheesy commencement speaker calls it "the real world"). It starts with an eager young man clutching his diploma and excitedly diving into what is promised to be an "up and coming" job opportunity.

After only one month, his story takes a leap off the side of a cliff like Thelma and Louise driving into oblivion. He finds himself in a web of deceit and manipulation because his boss has the morals of a Third World dictator. The boy with the promising, enviable job winds up spending his days lying to clients, paying fees for his boss' bounced paychecks, and generally wallowing in the lowest circles of Hell until he has a nervous breakdown at twenty-three.

"Oh come on, grow a pair, it couldn't really be that bad," you say.

Allow me to illustrate. I call this my Top 5 (but trust

me, there are at least 5,000) "Holy F—n Crap, You Must Be Kidding Me!" moments from my first job after college:

9/11/2001. I worked in Washington, D.C., and our office overlooked a main thoroughfare. On that awful day the street was filled with gridlocked cars and panicked people running and screaming—it was pandemonium. As my boss and I looked out at the chaos from our office window, he handed me a stack of business cards and ordered me to go hand them out to everyone stuck in traffic since it was "a great opportunity for business." (Mind you, the company was a graphics design and printing firm.) When I declined, he told me to "Stop being such a bitch."

Paydays can be tricky. In our small office of six (including our evil dictator), there was routinely only enough money for five people to be paid come payday—including Stalin himself. This was an unspoken but well-known fact. So the first five to get to the bank before it closed on Friday were the lucky ones. The latecomer had to wait until Monday when our boss could funnel money into the account from wherever else he was hiding it. He would often hand us our checks at 6:00 P.M. on Fridays, after the banks closed, or in sealed envelopes so we could not see they were unsigned, which apparently the banks have a big problem with.

Ticket to ride. After bouncing employees' checks on a fairly regular basis, my boss told me one day—quite proudly—

that he was buying his wife a Mercedes SUV. This was after he made me drive him around in my beat-up piece of junk for nine hours and pay for gas.

Burning the midnight oil. One day a massive job came in and my boss couldn't resist the money. So he had a co-worker and me work from 9:00 A.M. to 7:00 A.M.—that's twenty-two hours straight. After that shift, he benevolently said that I could go home, get some rest, and come back in around noon . . . the same day.

The tax man. After I quit the job, my boss failed to deliver my W2 tax form on time because he was too busy fixing his books with his crooked accountant, which forced me to file late. And when the W2 finally arrived, it was incorrect.

Why am I telling you all this?

These examples of my first foray into "the real world" are not meant to scare you. Okay, maybe a little. The reason why I'm sharing these horror stories is so you know that I've been in your shoes. Sure, I hope you don't have as dodgy a start as I did in your career, but I guarantee that most of us will have (or have had) to wade through troubled waters to achieve professional success, no matter how you define it. Plus, how could I understand and resolve improper business behavior if I never experienced it—at massive levels—for the majority of my career?

Like so many other graduates, I thought that my career

would take a traditional, linear path. I figured I'd go to college, get a degree, land a job, and stick with that field until Social Security kicked in. I mean, let's face it, this is real life, not the movies. I'm not going to sit down at Starbucks next to some random person who just so happens to be a CEO who says, "Son, I can just tell you have potential. How would you like a job?" Also, like many other young people, I thought the world was waiting for my ideas and when I got that degree, the gates of good fortune would fly open. (Cue the *Rocky* theme.)

That's not how it went. And trust me, it's not how it will ever go.

The days of a simple path from college to retirement do not exist anymore. Nowadays it's pretty normal for people to transition to different professions at least a few times in their working life. This requires you to hustle, to make yourself as marketable as possible. Think of a shark. A shark requires constant motion to survive. If it stops moving, it dies. That's how you have to be—bending, learning, adapting—and if you don't operate that way, the other predators in the ocean will have you for breakfast.

Speaking of predators, let's go back to that hellhole in D.C. Since I didn't know any better, I could have easily stayed at that crappy job with my tyrant of a boss and allowed my ass to get handed to me for the next thirty years. I *could* have. But I didn't.

Am I grateful for that terrible walk through Satan's playground after college? *Hell no!* Come on, people, have you been following at all? That was torture! I prayed for that benevolent CEO to come my way out of the blue. But again, we all know that isn't how it works.

I still remember the day I quit that job. I thought for sure it was going to come to blows. After all, my boss was a spoiled egomaniac, who didn't see anything wrong with the day-to-day operations (rob, cheat, lie, repeat). A person with that mentality looks at people disagreeing with him—let alone quitting—as the highest form of disrespect, so I expected him to lash out. I chose to tell him at lunchtime as I figured he'd be happier on a full stomach. We walked outside and I said, "Look, I don't think this is working for me and I'm giving my two weeks' notice now." I balled my fists in my pockets, waiting for him to charge me or take a swing. To my utter surprise (and slight disappointment), his only response was a simple "Okay." Then he walked away and that was the last time we spoke. Turns out, he was as much of a wimp as he was a liar. The day I left, I got a handshake and a cheesy grin good-bye. That was it. A bridge was burned, but I made it out unscathed.

I left that first job thinking it was always going to be that bad. I expected that all bosses would be rude and ignorant, that employees would be mere pawns, not key players. I was wrong, and I admit that the chip on my shoulder that was planted by my first job gets smaller and smaller every day. It's still there, though; it always will be. I think that's what moves me forward: if you have a chip, it means you have something to prove. So I wear it proudly, but don't let it affect how I conduct myself as a professional.

No grudges, no regrets.

That was twelve years ago.

Since then, my career has gone in a variety of unexpected directions, all of which led to the writing of this book. Granted I'm not on *Forbes'* list of richest CEOs, but when it comes to a life of the most careers, I'm definitely a contender. I've gone from being a professional wrestler (my stage name was "The Thrill From Israel" Buster Maccabi—true story!), to hosting a manners-and-etiquette podcast that is heard by millions of people in more than 200 countries around the world. Quite a different path from what I originally planned, to say the least!

In between these two careers, I've launched an award-winning Internet magazine, wrote and illustrated a series of popular children's books, invented a fashion accessory, and launched my own children's clothing line called Charm City Babies. Turns out, I have an entrepreneurial streak. I never would have known that if I didn't take a series of flying leaps into the unknown. Has it been easy? Not even a little. But even with the speed bumps I can honestly say that I prefer the more chaotic ride to the linear and mundane.

In 2010 I was approached by the editor of Macmillan's

Quick and Dirty Tips (a popular Web site and podcasting network) to become Modern Manners Guy. I would create a weekly column and podcast about manners in the twenty-first century. This was a dream come true! I would get to use my personal experience to help others tackle their daily struggles in this super-connected, privacy-free digital world. It turns out that all those awful people and situations I've encountered in my varied career would give me the tools I needed to help others overcome their own trials. How could I say no, right?

Nowadays, because of my role as Modern Manners Guy, I'm routinely invited to appear on TV, print, and radio outlets to tell my story and share the lessons I've learned over the years about how our behavior can directly affect our career successes and failures. It turns out that people dig the idea of a five-foot-five guy from the suburbs of Baltimore going from the gritty underworld of pro wrestling to the classier side of life. But let's get real: this is the twenty-first century and I'm not a scion of Emily Post, which is why you won't find advice on folding napkins or party planning in this book.

I have a freakish photographic memory, so when I tell you that I remember the exact moment something happened, you can believe it really went that way. Like the day I got the e-mail about the opportunity to write this book.

I was checking my in-box as my daughter played with

a puzzle on the floor of the pediatrician's office. Suddenly, my editor's name appeared with the subject line ARE YOU READY? And there it was. I got the green light.

First, I stood to my feet and screamed a gigantic "YESSSSS!," followed by a few colorful expletives. It wasn't a "Yes, this will be a splendid opportunity." No, it was more like the "Yes" a boxer or MMA fighter feels after a knockout—a teeth-grating, fist-squeezing, kiss-your-own-bicep-as-you-flex kind of "Yes!" This was the culmination of a dream I'd carried throughout my professional life. Now I could share the unspoken rules of success with millions! Now I could stop others from making the mistakes that could permanently compromise their careers.

But after I calmed down and apologized to the other parents in the waiting room for teaching their toddlers some new choice words, I was hit with the startling realization that I had to do something different. Writing the same ho-hum advice you've read again and again about how it's polite to say thank you in a job interview or show up on time wasn't the point. I wanted to do something much more relevant and real, something that pulled back the veil of corporate life and showed the underbelly. I wanted to reveal the insider info that we all wish the top dogs would tell us *before* we screwed up.

So I went straight to the top. I contacted leaders in a variety of industries, from fashion to technology, from restaurants to real estate, from Wall Street to Hollywood. I wanted my readers to hear firsthand from the elite that they too had it rough in the beginning—and even more important, I wanted to reveal how they succeeded where countless others failed. It was a huge responsibility.

Or as my editor put it, "Don't screw this up!"

Got it.

So I thought back to the day I decided to leave my awful first job. What if I never found anything better? What if all bosses were there to push me around? What if all coworkers were gargoyles who got under my skin? What if I couldn't afford rent or food? I wish it was easier, or that my first job was my immediate ticket to success, but it wasn't and in the end, I'm glad. Sometimes we need a little fear to push us to jump without a net. Like the first time I jumped off the top ropes in a wrestling ring; I had no idea what it would feel like when I landed but I knew I'd get back up. This is what every CEO, entrepreneur, and entertainer I interviewed for this book told me. Not one person said their life turned out the way they thought it would and absolutely no one had it easy (not even the people with the financial edge). They all agreed that in the end, only your character and the way you treat others will get you what you want.

And even if you burn bridges, don't be the one to light the match.

Loveland Public Library
Loveland, CO

Job Interview Etiquette

Hello world, I'm here! World? . . . Hello? . . . Your diploma is a piece of paper, not a magic wand.

> You can be born rich, but you can't be born successful!
> —Richie Frieman, Modern Manners Guy

I love this quote for many reasons. For one, it's probably the single best reminder of how the real world works. Secondly, it's also something people tend to forget when starting a job. If it were up to me, this slogan would be plastered on the wall of every college classroom as a reminder that the real world—especially the professional world—is not someplace where you can simply rely on luck or your personal heritage to get you by.

Now, by "rich" I'm not talking about money. I'm talking about the idea that just because you were born into something or handed an opportunity, it automatically makes you a success. Success is *earned,* not given out like a free cake on your birthday or for reaching Gold status at Starbucks.

Sure, you can have help getting in the door (I recommend it!), but once you're in, you are on your own. Which school you went to, who you know, or how much money you or your parents have all take a backseat to what you can accomplish with your own two hands and that thing that sits right between your ears. Nothing trumps hard work. Period.

This chapter is filled with quotes, stories, and anecdotes from influential people in a wide variety of industries, all of whom have their own theories on what makes a person successful—from the way you present yourself, to the way you work with others, to how you travel, behave at meetings and dinners, and many other situations that shape the success (or failure) of your career. Those who rely on the achievements of others will never make it (I'm talking to you silver spooners!). Success is not like a hand-me-down piece of clothing that fits great on one person, so the next will look equally good. You can't give someone success in a pretty little box and expect them to maintain it once the box is open. Sadly, this simple truth is often lost on people who allow their egos to get the better of them.

Say it with me: "The world doesn't owe me anything."

In this chapter, I will take you on a tour of the ever-nerve-racking job interview, as seen from both sides of the table. So before you forget to iron that new shirt, arrive late to the interview because your alarm didn't go off, and say "Hey, man!" when you shake the interviewers' hand,

"Look, if it worked for Zuckerberg, it works for me.
So, about that salary . . ."

check out my dos, don'ts, and please-don't-evers of proper job interview etiquette.

There is a reason why job interviews make people nervous. You *should* be nervous. It's a big deal. After interviewing a long list of industry bigwigs for this book, I've learned that they start reading (and judging) you the moment you walk into their office. Job interviews go way past your résumé, or the fancy college diploma you have hanging over your bed. The interview starts the moment you open the door. Every second is a test. And like a test, many people fail.

But the good news is that like a test, you can study for your job interview—and yes, even cram until the last minute—to make sure you are prepared. However, a job interview is different in that it's not for a grade, it's to see if you are really as sharp as your diploma says you are.

The Pros Weigh In: BARBARA CORCORAN
**Real estate mogul, investor, and resident shark
on ABC's hit show *Shark Tank***

• • •

Millions of people tune in each week to watch Barbara Corcoran take a bite out of investment seekers on ABC's *Shark Tank*. On the show, budding entrepreneurs vie for attention with only minutes to make a good impression on the sharks who can fund their dreams. Little do they know that before they even finish their first sentence, Barbara has already made a gut call.

Harsh?

Absolutely.

But it's not just manufactured drama for TV. When it comes to business, many people (aka, the ones doing the hiring) use their gut instinct to judge the people they meet. Barbara told me about one particular situation when a job applicant came into her office for an interview:

We have a fairly small office with a staff of only six or seven people. So when you walk inside, you immediately see the workplace of the entire group. This job applicant came in early and the first thing he said to my assistant was: 'I'm here for an ap-

pointment with Mrs. Corcoran. Would you rather I wait outside?' Outside? It was raining outside . . . I love this guy! He walked in, realized that he might be interrupting, and acted on it immediately so that we weren't inconvenienced— even though he had an appointment. Great, great move. I hired that guy. It was almost as if everything he said after that point was prejudice against the positive. I saw him through rosy lenses through the next hour and a half that I talked with him.

> **Whether or not the person likes you is going to be decided within the first five or six seconds of your meeting.**
> —Barbara Corcoran, founder of The Corcoran Group and investor on ABC's *Shark Tank*

This story points out one clear fact about interviewing for the job—you are not hired yet. You have to *earn* that spot. When you step onto their turf, you have to swallow some humble pie and appreciate every second of their time. It's foolish to assume that you have any advantage over another candidate. Sure, sometimes you may share a mutual contact that got you the interview, or your dad plays golf with the CFO on the weekends, but at the end of the day a manager wants to hire the best person for the job. If you march in thinking you already own the place, it will surely be the end of the interview.

As Barbara says:

Whether or not the person likes you is going to be decided within the first five or six seconds of your meeting. So you really better watch what you say and do in those first moments. I very rarely change my opinion after that initial five or six seconds. You sit down, you exchange cordialities, and usually the person doing the interview has decided if they like you. They might not have decided if they're going to hire you yet, but they've decided if they like you. So you have to be very polished and think through how you come across. A lot of people think they have a warm-up period, but that's really not true. The biggest impression you can never take back is those first few seconds.

I know what you're thinking: "What the hell! Five or six seconds? I'm still freaking out about even being interviewed! And making sure my fly is zipped! How is this fair?"

Well, life's not fair and job interviews are a huge part of your professional life. So you better figure out how to make those moments count.

Thankfully, you don't have to go it alone!

The day of your job interview, I recommend pretending you are on camera from the minute you leave your house to the minute you come back home. This sounds bizarre but it's a practice for the big show, which should be the only thing on your mind. Because if you are not focused solely on winning over the interviewer that day, it will take a heck of a lot to fix that first impression.

Modern Manners Guy's Top 10 Tips for Job-Interview Etiquette

Tip #1: Recon and Research

You finally landed an interview, but before you step foot in the office, you need to make sure you will look the part you are applying for. But how do you know how to look like you're the only one for the job without ever having met your future coworkers? For this, I recommend doing a little recon and research.

Recon? Yes, recon.

Simply put, scope out the company before your interview. During a regular workday, swing by the office and simply watch as people walk in, either from your car or just stroll by. But don't wear a hoodie and dark sunglasses like some freaky pervert hiding outside your ex's house. Just act normal. Hold a coffee and your smartphone to blend in. Use this time to observe people walking into your future workplace for a half hour or so. Take notes on what they wear and if they carry a messenger bag or backpack.

For the interview, you'll need to take it to the next level. So if your new coworkers wear only dress shirts and casual slacks, then you'll wear a sharp suit. If they carry messenger bags, you'll bring the nicest one you can find. If they use a briefcase, go get one. You don't even have to buy one at this point, just borrow a friend's or family member's for the day.

As well, spend some time on the Web site to see how the company views itself . . . which ultimately means how they want their employees to be viewed. Most company sites feature an About Us page that shows information about the employees, if not photos of their office. See how they present themselves and take note. Whatever you do, do not try and flaunt what your momma gave you or wear a flashy outfit. Stick to classic, elegant, understated. No Lycra, no loud colors, and all parts of the body that would take a movie from PG-13 to R should be covered.

Tip #2: Don't Be Late

> If you're early, you're on time. If you're on time, you're late. If you're late, don't bother showing up.
> —Vince Lombardi, Pro Football Hall of Fame coach

A job interview should be the single most important part of your day. If something else is taking that priority spot, then chances are you will not be the best candidate for the position. Employers want commitment, not someone who thinks being a few minutes late is acceptable. It isn't. Ever. If you live far away, leave early to avoid traffic or public transportation snafus. "My train was delayed" is a juvenile excuse and you won't be taken seriously.

When you leave the meeting, you need to also leave a lasting memory with your interviewer. And if you think being late is okay, they will remember that. Don't ever think that you're the only person being considered for the job. There is always someone else in the mix. So when it comes down to it, the details are what will make or break your chances. And speaking of details . . .

Tip #3: Details *Do* Matter

Have you ever been to a party and met someone you liked and wanted to see again? For whatever reason, this person made an impression on you. But what kind of lasting impression did you leave on them? Did they remember that you too love karaoke? Did they remember that you both clicked on digging bad 1980s movies?

Well, the same thing goes for a job interview. When you leave their office, you need to ask yourself, "Was I memorable?" After all, in a sea of possible candidates, you have to stand out from the rest. Even if you think your diploma is the best in the world, chances are that's not what the interviewer will remember. So what will they remember? The details.

Here's how to make yourself stand out: During the interview, pick out something in the interviewer's office and comment on it when there's a lull in the conversation. That photo of him on a boat? Ask about sailing. The golf club leaning up against her desk? Ask how often or where she plays. A photo of kids or dogs? Ask how old or what breed they are (respectively). People love talking about their pets and kids so this is a guaranteed icebreaker. Choose something personal and then see where the conversational thread goes. Just one little question or action will make you more personable and memorable in a field of equally qualified (but unremarkable) candidates.

Tip #4: Dress for the Job You Want

> The first impression will dominate regardless of how often it is contradicted by new experiences.
> —Dr. Bertram Gawronski, social psychologist and author

A job interview is not the red carpet, but looking put together and professional is still critical. No one will ask you, "Who are you wearing?" And if they do ask you, and base their decision on your answer, then you don't want to work there anyway. (The only exception: If you're interviewing at a fashion company, then any fashion labels you're wearing may actually play a role in the decision. Otherwise, nine times out of ten, as long as you look well dressed and polished, that's the deal maker.)

According to noted author and social psychologist Dr.

Bertram Gawronski, nothing you can do can take back that initial first impression:

> *Imagine you have a new colleague at work and your impression of that person is not very favorable. A few weeks later, you meet your colleague at a party and you realize he is actually a very nice guy. Although you know your first impression was wrong, your gut response to your new colleague will be influenced by your new experience only in contexts that are similar to the party. However, your first impression will still dominate in all other contexts.*

Let's be honest, we do judge people by that initial first impression. You remember that blind date where the guy shows up wearing his "Everything's Bigger in Texas" T-shirt with an arrow pointing to his crotch? I'm guessing you weren't thinking, "Oh, what a catch!" Well, that same thing happens in the professional world. Your job interview is essentially a blind date and it's up to you to woo the interviewer and make them fall in love with you.

So when you walk into that meeting, you can guarantee that you are being judged right away. This does not mean you have to look like the cover of *GQ* or *Vogue* and splurge on a $5,000 custom suit. You do, however, need to take time to evaluate your appearance before you leave your house. This goes double for all you Mark Zuckerberg wannabes who think your flip-flops and zip-up hoodies say, "I'm a laid-back guy, just going with the flow," or the nonconformists who think wearing a suit means you've sold out. What it really means is that you'll look like a fool if you are not actively trying to impress your future employer. Sure, Zuckerberg can get away with it—he's a billionaire founder of a game-changing company. If he wants to dress like the Easter Bunny every day, he can. You, the one who is trying to land a new job, cannot.

If the interview goes well and you get hired, you will be a representative of the company both in and out of the office, so by looking the part during the interview, you show to that employer that you can make them look good. Every industry has its own unique style, which you will discover during your recon mission (see Tip #1) and paying proper attention to that is one surefire way to impress your future employer.

Tip #5: Iron Out the Details

What you wear says volumes. It shows how serious you are, it shows respect for the job and the interviewer, and it gets you ready to perform.
—Vince Rua, founder/CEO of Christopher's Custom and president of Suits For The Cause, Inc.

Regardless of how expensive or budget-friendly your outfit is, you'll always impress your potential employer by looking ironed, creased, and pristine. Choose your interview outfit ahead of time and send it to the cleaners to get a good press. And don't go the night before expecting it to be ready the morning of the interview. That's cutting it way too close. Manners go far beyond just what you say and how you act; it's also a visual language. So when it comes to that job interview—whether it's how you dress, smell, or comb your hair—always sweat the small stuff.

> Showing up to a job interview poorly dressed, with messy hair, a wrinkled shirt, and/or mismatched clothes can reveal many things about you—from a lack of discipline or order in life, to just not taking the prospect of working at the employer seriously.
> —Pranav Vora, founder of Hugh & Crye

One guy I used to work with took looking disheveled to an art form. It wasn't just what he wore or how he smelled—neither of which was good—this guy was consistently wrinkled to a point that it looked like his clothes were made of tissue paper and then balled up into the fists of a very mad person who used them as stress relief. Look, wrinkles happen—especially while you're in the car, the train, or even just carrying a shoulder bag—but if you choose your fabrics wisely and take the time to look crisp and creased, your future boss will notice.

Tip #6: Eye Contact

As a person who has dealt with ADHD his entire life, I'll admit I have a hard time slowing down my racing mind and maintaining eye contact. But when it matters, such as when I'm shooting a TV segment or interviewing celebrities, I make sure I'm on point and looking straight at the person I'm talking to. At a job interview, this is especially critical. Looking away when you speak, fidgeting in your seat, peppering your conversation with parasite words ("like," "you know," "umm," "I mean," etc.) tells them you are not comfortable and possibly inarticulate. And if you can't be comfortable in front of them, you will never be comfortable in front of clients or in a meeting with a large audience.

Keeping eye contact with the person in front of you is a surefire way to exude confidence and composure.

Try this: The next time you meet a friend for coffee or lunch, count how many times their eyes go away from you during that time. You'll begin to pick up on how annoying and distracting that can be to a conversation. While you're at it, try and keep a tally of how many times your friend uses parasite words. I bet you'll lose track after a minute or so. Once you start focusing on these words, you'll see how irritating they are.

Tip #7: Check Your Ego at the Door

By far one of the biggest mistakes you can make during a job interview is assuming you already have the job. When you're applying for a position, you're not in the driver's seat. Granted, you could be the smartest, slickest, most dynamic person ever to grace the earth, but you must not act like it. Not only will the interviewer see right through you, they'll also feel patronized and played and will probably think you're an ass. Oftentimes, people mistake arrogance for confidence. I can guarantee you that acting like you're the cat's meow will come across as annoying at best and patronizing at worst.

The Pros Weigh In: STEVE ABRAMS
Entrepreneur and CEO of Magnolia Bakery

• • •

Steve Abrams is a tough guy. I learned that the minute we started talking and I asked him about his career which, as he says, "went from construction to cupcakes." He started out in the hard-nosed construction and development business where attitudes, arguments, and egos were the norm. So when Abrams switched to cupcakes, purchasing the famous Magnolia Bakery, he was happy for the change in scenery and personalities. I mean, it's cupcakes—who can't help but smile when hearing the word "cupcake," right? I'm smiling right now!

Abrams says that regardless of the industries he entered or people he met with, he was able to crack their tough exterior to get down to business. It's just about finding the common ground and making that connection— key elements during a job interview, or the initial business meeting for sure.

I'm pretty comfortable with people in general. If you are meeting someone new, in their office, it's easy to look around and see if there is a common interest. They might have kids, they might play sports, they might have awards. The approach is different depending on the nature of the business you are doing.

Even though Abrams says he's quick to find that comfort in any situation, he's not so quick to tolerate someone whose ego is already ten feet in front of them when they walk through the door. In any job interview, you are being tested and any time an executive like Abrams has someone come to sell themselves or their product, they better be ready to react on the fly.

I'm not the kind of executive who has the time for the forty-minute Power Point. The minute you pull that out, you've lost me. Tell me what you're going to do and do it. I don't like a lot of chatter around it if I don't need it. You should be able to talk extemporaneously about the product and your services. If it takes that long you're trying to over-complicate it or confuse me—purposely or not. I tend to take people off guard when someone walks in with this kind of presentation and I don't allow them to do it. It will tell me how they think on their feet, and also how they act in adversity.

> Being inexperienced and at the same time arrogant is not going to get you too far. You have to be willing to learn and put in the hard work. That's how you can improve your knowledge and skills and learn to work well with others, which are key for success.
> —Jonathan Monaghan, artist and animator

Tip #8: Don't Overdo the Cologne or Perfume

We've all been in a situation when we're approached by someone who is wearing enough "smell good" to last a month. And we all remember what a huge turnoff that is. Same thing goes for a job interview. You want to overwhelm the room with your qualifications, not your scent. Nothing should distract the boss from your résumé, including your odor—good or bad.

Don't get me wrong, you should definitely wear something to make yourself smell nice. But do it subtly so that you're not left smelling like you took a Calvin Klein bath. The minute you do that, your potential employer will notice it and they'll think "I can't send this person to a client meeting," and even worse, "I am going to have to smell this person every day." When it comes to scents, stick to two sprays of cologne or perfume. I'd even say spritz the second one into the air and then walk into it to minimize the damage.

Tip #9: The Sign-Off

When an interview is winding down, it's similar to being on a date. Who is going to make the first move to ask for date #2? How many of you have returned home from a date and kicked yourself simply because you were too shy to ask, "Can I see you again?" Ending the job interview works in a similar way. And if you don't make an effort to set that next date, you'll likely stay up late, waiting for that special someone to call or text—unsure if they will. Improperly closing an interview will leave you in a similar position.

Before you shake hands and part ways, you have to know what happens next. Not necessarily if you have the job, but when will you hear back. This is not bold or aggressive, it's simply professional. According to Barbara Corcoran:

> *I love an aggressive, polite close. It's the final chance for the applicant to earn my respect. And the perfect close is, "I really appreciate your time. When will I hear from you regarding this position?" If I interview someone and they leave and I haven't given them an idea about when I'll get back to them, they're not aggressive enough for me—in any job. That said, be careful not to go too aggressive as it can backfire. I have someone who works for me, a writer, and writers tend to*

be pretty introverted. After the interview, she asked me point blank, "Do I have the job?" A little rude for some people, but I had to respect her for it. It's an important closure question. It says, "I respect my own time."

Tip #10: The Perfect Thank-You

In a highly digital world, most people assume that a simple e-mail "Thank You" does the job. And yes, that's the fastest thing to do. And faster can also mean the easiest or the most expected. But being one in the pool of many, you have to stand out. That's why I recommend doing something bold: handwrite a letter. The handwritten thank-you note in business has become retro. It's like meeting someone with a vinyl record player in the house.

When you receive a letter, you think, "Wow, I haven't seen one of those in years!" (or maybe ever) and that's what you want. You want to be noticed, to stick out from the mass of applicants, to show that you took the time to compose something personal. Anyone can type out a thank-you e-mail during the walk to their car after the interview, but you have to put in a certain amount of time and attention to the act of writing. That means a lot to the recipient of your note. Plus, it turns out that an e-mailed thank-you may not even reach your intended recipient. Check out what Barbara Corcoran says:

People think that a CEO or boss will always get your e-mails. This is not true. Most of the time, my assistant gets my e-mail. So she may not forward that "Thank You" from someone and I'll never see it. But if you send me a handwritten note, that will always land on my desk. That's what makes you memorable.

Don't worry if you aren't the type of person who has your own letterhead. Any note, handwritten on a simple card is a lot better than the generic "Thanks for your time" email. When purchasing the card, stick to something simple and clean. Nothing spiritual, religious, or political. Nothing too funny or cloying. And definitely nothing sexual or laced with innuendo. An added bonus is if you are from out of town and send them a thank you card that is from your city, since that probably came up in the interview. Always mail your note the same day of the interview. They will see the stamped date on it and that will earn you even more bonus points.

The Pros Weigh In: VINCE RUA
Founder/CEO of Christopher's Custom
and president of Suits for the Cause

• • •

Dress to impress. There's no set way to dress for every workplace. It all depends on the dynamics of the office. A good rule of thumb is to dress in the office so that you are prepared for any call to duty. You might be called to confer with a client, and that client might have on a suit, so you have to be ready. Keep a blazer in the office that looks acceptable over the outfit you are wearing. This takes some consideration, but you can find a navy or black blazer that can easily complement almost any ensemble. If you're in sales, you should dress one level above the prospect. If the prospect is wearing jeans and a T-shirt, you should wear neatly pressed pants or skirt and dress shirt. If the prospect wears business casual, you should wear a blazer or suit.

MODERN MANNERS GUY QUIZ

You walk into a job interview and find out that everyone in the office is wearing a three-piece suit and you are dressed business casual. What do you do?

A Panic! Run outside screaming mad at yourself.

B Go on with the interview and over-apologize for not dressing "up to par," making sure they know that you will ramp it up once you start working there.

C Ask to reschedule the interview so you can better prepare.

D Feel confident that you have a backup blazer/jacket in the car to throw on at the last minute.

Answer

D I recommend always having backup dress clothes on hand at all times. Keep a spare shirt, blazer, and pants or a skirt in your car (and once you land the job, keep a set in your desk as well). Stick with neutral colors like black, gray, or navy. You never know when you're going to spill or tear something before a big meeting. By having a backup, you will be able to keep your cool and remain calm, when others may panic.

The job interview is not the time to apologize for your appearance. The more you dwell on it, the more they will too and the interview focus will shift from your qualifications to what you did wrong. Just ignore it and move on.

MODERN MANNERS GUY'S JOB INTERVIEW TOOL KIT

1 PACK A CHANGE OF CLOTHES. Always have a spare pair of pants, a shirt, and a blazer, just in case you spill something or if the weather is bad. Keep them folded neatly in the trunk of your car or in your bag.

② ALWAYS CARRY A BAG. Women, you have it easy. For you, bringing a bag to hold the essentials tends to be the norm. That's not the case for many guys. But whatever job you're applying for, always bring a briefcase or a messenger bag to the interview. If you don't have one, borrow one from a friend or family member. Make sure it's in good shape, and not the crappy one you used as a pillow during college study breaks in the library. This not only makes you look professional, but it also allows you the chance to store away your wallet, keys, papers, cell phone, etc. You don't want your pockets looking like you're trying to sneak snacks into a movie theater. That just screams "amateur."

③ PACK SOME SMELL GOOD. Yes, I said not to overdo the cologne, but a lot can be said for showing up to an interview after having walked ten blocks in the heat of summer smelling like . . . well, like you walked ten blocks in the heat of summer. To avoid this, keep a small travel-size bottle of cologne and deodorant in your bag at all times.

④ PACK BREATH MINTS/GUM. I doubt anyone has ever said, "Wow, that guy's breath smelled way too good!" But I will guarantee you they've said that it smelled bad. Keep mints and/or gum on you at all times. Don't ever go into the meeting chewing anything, but make sure you use breath freshener within five minutes of the interview and throw it away before you go inside.

⑤ THANK-YOU NOTES. A handwritten thank-you note can quickly put a "Maybe" candidate into the "Yes" column. Before you go into the interview, bring a note and a stamped envelope with you. When you're done with the meeting, fill out the card and mail it the same day. That way, it will arrive within a day or two of your meeting and solidify the good impression you left with the interviewer.

TWO

First Day on the Job

Why your first day on the job could be your most important—and your last.

> By working faithfully eight hours a day you may eventually get to be boss and work twelve hours a day.
> —Robert Frost, writer and poet

Regardless of who I speak to, the story is the same. Whether they dove headfirst into a new job the day after college graduation or took a few months off to "find themselves," they walked into a new job for the first time feeling energized, empowered, ready to tackle the world. Then, later that night, when they crashed from exhaustion onto their couch, they were left wondering what they'd gotten themselves into.

I'm not saying this to scare you—OK, maybe a little. However, this is the reality of your first day on the job. You may think you know everything about the company— after all, you did become a fan on Facebook—but what you saw at the job interview was more of a show. Not that they were faking it, but the interview is the "get to know you" time, not the "this is what it's really like" time. That's why day one at your new job can be revelatory (and sometimes, a letdown).

I'm not sure when this will happen to you, but undoubtedly sometime during that first day, you'll find yourself staring blankly at your computer screen in your new slice of corporate office dwelling, wondering, "What now . . . ?"

Don't worry. Having been through this wild ride of the first day many times over, I can tell you there is hope. You can make it through the first day unscathed and without feeling like you'll be fired on day two.

In this chapter, I'll give you examples of situations you may encounter on your first day, along with tips on how to successfully handle them so that you always come out on top. It doesn't matter where you work or who you work for, your first day on the job will be more of an uphill hike than a red carpet stroll. It won't be bad, necessarily, but like anything new, it's going to be a challenge. There's a lot to take in, but don't think of this as a system overload; rather as a system refresh. So before you get lost on the way to your desk, mispronounce the name of your new boss, get stuck figuring out the phone system, or spill coffee all over your new (and only) pair of dress pants, check out my first day dos and don'ts.

The Pros Weigh In: MICHAEL WEINSTEIN
Former CEO of Snapple and COO of
A&W Root Beer, aka "The Beverage Guy"

• • •

While conducting the interviews you'll find throughout this book, one thing that I heard consistently was the fact that the first day on the job caused more nausea and stress than any other aspect of professional life—even more than the interview process itself (see chapter 1).

That first day on the job, you are on display; you are the "newbie." And as the new (and probably low) man or woman on the totem pole, you'll need to conquer your first day so it won't be your last.

One guy who knows a thing or two about being the new guy is former CEO of Snapple and COO of A&W Root Beer, Michael Weinstein. Weinstein has been revolutionizing the beverage industry since he first took a job with Pepsi-Cola in 1972. While talking with Weinstein, I learned many things about what it takes to succeed in business through the eyes of a man whose personality is bolder than the lip-smacking flavors he helped create over the years. Not one to hold back his opinions, Weinstein was very clear about the one thing that would get you booted from the job:

> *I was legendary at Snapple for my obsession with having people show up on time. In fact, my office overlooked the parking lot and sometimes people*

would park far away and come in the back door so I wouldn't catch them coming in late. The truth is that I saved my wrath for the people who were late every day—usually with excuses like "I live far away and hit traffic" or "The school bus was late and I had to wait with my kid." To the traffic guys I said, "If you hit traffic every day, maybe it's time to realize that if you leave earlier, you can get here on time." And for childcare issues, I always proposed the option of changing start (and consequently end) times of a person's workday. When you try to build a team, it's really important that all teammates follow the rules together or discord can occur.

Your first day at a new company is not just new for you—there is a learning curve on both sides. And it starts the minute you walk in the door. Inevitably there will be personalities you encounter at work that will challenge your patience. But as Weinstein says:

Find a profession that you love, but a company that your personality fits into. Just like people, each company has a distinct personality (some are assholes, some are warm and caring, some are passive, some are aggressive, etc.). If you can match your personality to that of the organization, you have your best chance of success.

And success starts on day one. If you think otherwise, or think the first day is simply a welcome party, you are wrong. Very wrong.

> In the corporate world, you're balancing how to fit in and stand out at the same time. You want to contribute as a team player, yet get noticed for the good work you do. No matter what your first project or assignment is, make sure you hit it out of the park. Your work ethic, capabilities, and overall worth are quickly assessed in the first few interactions with peers and senior folks. Make sure you work your butt off for the first one, as your impact (or lack thereof) will follow you in subsequent projects.
> —Pranav Vora, founder of Hugh & Crye

Modern Manners Guy's Top 10 Tips for Your First Day on the Job

Tip #1: Show Up Early

Take a chapter out of the Michael Weinstein playbook—punctuality does matter. A lot. Being on time is highly underrated and yet, it's the thing that truly gets under people's skin. When you're late, you're basically telling people waiting for you that your life takes precedence over theirs. It's rude, unprofessional, and the fastest way to a bad first impression (see chapter 1).

For your first day at work, you should be early. I'm not

saying you have to camp out like those teenagers who waited in line for the latest *Twilight* premiere, but I highly recommend arriving *before* the time they asked you to. If everyone starts the day at 9:00 A.M., arrive at 8:45 A.M. There is no excuse why you can't do this. If you get there too early, simply have some breakfast at a coffee shop close by, or just stay in your car and surf the Web on your smartphone.

To ensure that you can arrive on time, I recommend doing a test run of an actual workday prior to starting your job. Wake up and get ready as if you were going to work and leave at the time that you figure will be sufficient for getting there promptly. See how traffic goes, what the delays may be, and adjust your actual commuting time accordingly. This way, you don't wake up in a panic on day one and blast curses at strangers because you got delayed by traffic or public transportation snafus.

There are two things that your early arrival will demonstrate to the Powers That Be—both of which are good:

1. That you have respect for the job.
2. That you are responsible (aka, they can count on you).

Simply put, arriving promptly is a quality valued by every manager and CEO, even if they don't outright say it. It's like when the person you're dating says they don't really want a present for their birthday. They're lying. They do want a present. They just don't want to say it. Instead, they want you to figure it out on your own.

Tip #2: Introduce Yourself

On your first day at a new job, you have to be personable. I don't mean to suggest that you hop up on the conference room table and do a stand-up routine or send out an Evite for a happy hour after work, but you must be friendly. Even if you are not the biggest extrovert in the world, make an effort. Come out of your shell and be ready to chat it up with your new coworkers.

The first day plays a big role in the all-important first impression (see chapter 1) and the key is to present yourself as someone who will be a part of the team. When you walk in the door, everyone will know you are the newbie. If you look away, don't smile, hide your face by looking at the floor, or bury your nose in your smartphone, they will think you're rude. And doing all those things *is* rude, so they would be right.

Tip #3: Be Accessible

I'll never forget this one time my coworker Amy told our boss that she couldn't stay late because she had to attend a spin class. Now, I am all for fitness, but telling your boss that you can't stay late because you're trying to knock off a few calories is a big mistake. In the professional world, you will miss parties, dinners, and yes, *even* spin classes because of your job. It's just a part of life.

Work does not have to *be* your life but it is the way you make a living and having to pitch in every now and then is just part of the package.

When you are fresh in a new job you have to make sacrifices, and by telling your boss you can't help out you're making your commitment (or lack thereof) loud and clear. Granted, your boss doesn't own you and your time; however, prioritizing is key. If you have an important event one night, by all means stand up for yourself. But a spin class or a date probably doesn't qualify. And if you can't stay late, give your boss a good reason why (a death in the family, for instance) and do whatever you can to get as much done as possible before you leave.

When you say that you can't devote some extra time to your work, you're sending a message that you're not a team player. This is a terrible way to kick-start your career. In your first job, you need to earn your stripes and that means making yourself accessible. It doesn't mean being at their beck and call *Devil Wears Prada*–style, but it does mean going above and beyond sometimes.

On day one, let your boss and your team know that you are there to help. If someone could use a hand with a project, make your willingness to take on more responsibility heard. The counter to this argument is that you do not want to become a Welcome mat for everyone to walk over. But there's not much threat of that in your first few days on the job. You'll have plenty of time to say "No" down the line and people will respect you for it. But if you start off immediately making yourself unavailable to your team, they will not count on you for bigger projects and the boss will not give you more responsibility, which would not lead to increased visibility within the company, which would not lead to promotions, raises, etc. You see where I'm going with this? Your automatic answer to just about any requests made by employers and colleagues on your first day is "Yes!"

Tip #4: Keep Busy

Most likely, you will not be inundated with a heavy workload on day one. Chances are, your day will be spent getting the lay of the land and figuring out what your role really is. If you find yourself looking for something to do, offer your services to someone on your team. Do not ask someone who is completely unrelated to your position. If you are in marketing, don't solicit work from the office manager, the intern, or someone in accounting. Find the people whom you'll be working with and shadow them for the day. You don't want anyone to find you in your cube keeping busy by creating new playlists on your iPod because you can't find anything to do. In a professional situation, there is always work to be done and sometimes you have to take some initiative. Along with lending a hand to a fellow team member, you'll also learn valuable lessons about the dynamics of your new workplace, and those are lessons best learned early.

Tip #5: Office Kitchen Etiquette

> Don't eat other people's food from the communal
> refrigerator . . . and don't leave your food
> there until it gets moldy.
> —Michael Weinstein, former CEO of Snapple
> and COO of A&W Root Beer

I've worked in offices that had full-blown state-of-the-art kitchens and in offices with a sad refrigerator and a rusty microwave that I'm convinced was used as the prototype by Sears in the 1980s. Whatever shape or size of your company's kitchen, it will inevitably be a gathering place for people to catch up, gossip, and sometimes actually talk shop. And as with any gathering place, there are many opportunities for disgusting displays of unmannerly behavior, which should be avoided at all costs. For some reason, the refrigerator and the microwave bring out the worst in people. So to make sure that you don't fall into one of these bad manners traps, let's take a closer look.

First, let's make one thing clear: Size *does* matter . . . when you're talking about refrigerators.

What did you think I meant?

Come on, get your head out of the gutter.

Just because a fridge is six feet tall and three feet wide, does not mean you can shove anything you like in there.

That leftover turkey from Thanksgiving still on its giant serving dish does *not* fit in the office fridge. You do not get a whole rack to yourself, you only get a small section. The easiest way to resolve this is to pack just for yourself, not for what you plan to prepare at lunch like a contestant on *Top Chef.* But there are some times when you need to bring in a larger dish, maybe for a holiday party or an event. In this case, simply ask in advance. Send an e-mail around to the team or the office manager and ask—do not tell—if it's OK for you to bring in something that will take up a large portion of the fridge.

The second major issue with the fridge is that people tend to forget they even put something in there, or they're too lazy to take it out. So the tuna salad that only has a two-day shelf life has now made friends with some green-and-brown mold and they're growing a colony. This is not an episode of *Hoarders*—if it's left in there too long, it gets dumped. Don't be surprised if someone dumps your left-over meat loaf because it's now liquefied into a gel-like mold.

The fridge's shorter, squatter partner in crime is the microwave. But it's just as bad when it comes to sanitation snafus. My first pet peeve about the microwave is when someone abandons their food in there like a sinking ship. Leaving your food in the microwave causes a negative ripple effect. Say you overheat your soup and it spills, leaving you to clean up the microwave mess. This makes your fellow coworkers wait even longer to use the appliance and grumble under their breath about how the new guy/girl is taking forever and they have work to do.

Second, I know this may be hard to hear but you are not the only one using the appliance. You saw the line of people behind you—did you think they just came to watch you? "Oh wow, Dave is heating up his spaghetti. Look at his technique . . ." Lunchtime is valuable and every second counts, including those wasted at the microwave. So get in, get out, and don't leave a mess. Don't be the guy or girl who makes everyone wait because you forgot your lunch in the microwave for half an hour.

Third, be careful about what sort of food you bring into the office kitchen. Yes, everyone has their own taste, but you have to be mindful of others. If the dish you brought for lunch has a strong odor, don't be surprised if your colleagues are gagging and complaining about the smell. And remember, stinky foods aren't just fish or meats; popcorn is notoriously odorous, especially if you burn it. The best way to show respect for your fellow coworkers is to cook something in the microwave with a neutral smell. Another thing to consider is that some people have strong allergies, so that even smelling a certain type of food will cause them to have a reaction. Do you want to be the one to cause Aaron in billing to go into anaphylactic shock because you microwaved leftover jambalaya?

The Pros Weigh In: ROB SAMUELS
COO of Maker's Mark

• • •

As I write this, I'm sipping on a cool glass of Maker's Mark and looking through a gorgeous book entitled *The Ambassador of Bourbon,* which tells the story of Maker's Mark. Rob Samuels was nice enough to give me the book as a gift (and it's autographed by him and founder Bill Samuels Sr.—I know, you're jealous!). And thank the Lord for spell check and my editor since the more time I spend with my cool glass, the more things blur together. Ahh, the taste of luscious Kentucky Bourbon Whisky . . . Okay, where was I? Oh that's right, drinking . . .

Let me start by saying that I truly admire Rob's career and how he got to where he is today. Yes, Maker's Mark is a family business and I'm sure most people would assume that Rob was guaranteed a job there from birth. However, this is not the case with Maker's Mark. In fact, Rob was a bit of a journeyman for many years before coming to Maker's Mark.

My father told me if I had interest in this industry to go to other companies, away from Kentucky. And I did that for eleven years. I was able to earn my stripes outside the shadows of Kentucky and Maker's Mark. But finally when I returned in 2006, it was nice to be welcomed home. I didn't want my father to feel like he had to hire his son.

After this eleven-year absence, Rob returned to Maker's Mark experienced and confident, ready to join the family business. His first day at work, he woke up fresh and ready to tackle his new position, he waved hello to people as he walked in, went into his father's office . . . and was fired that very morning.

> *True story: My first day at Maker's Mark I got there nice and early, had an office that was nothing more than a broom closet, and my dad came in with a cup of coffee. He says to me, "Okay, you're here, what good ideas do you have?" He caught me flat-footed. And I just blurted out, "I think we should advertise on television." He fired me right on the spot.*

Rob was shocked. Was this a test? Was he not supposed to have this job?

His father did hire him back shortly after dropping the bomb, but the lesson was that he had to be on his toes at all times. There are no shortcuts, no breaks, and no advantages—not even for the boss' son.

Tip #6: Taking Breaks

I'm a big supporter of taking breaks during the workday. Taking breaks not only allows people to de-stress, it also increases office morale. Whether it's a short walk around the building to catch a breath of fresh air, taking a few minutes to absorb some sunshine and call a friend, or even (gasp!) a smoke break, these are all necessities of office life.

Taking breaks definitely helped me get by at my first job out of college. I worked on the same block as a Starbucks, but I was not a coffee drinker at the time. However, as I passed by the cafe on my way to work, I couldn't help but be lured by its siren-like scents. As my love of coffee developed, my utter disgust for my new job also grew. And since I don't smoke and we weren't allowed to step outside for phone calls, going on coffee breaks was my only source of sanity.

What started as just me walking down the street for a quick cup turned into an exodus as my fellow coworkers—equally depressed—joined me for some cherished time away from the madness. That tiny slice of our day was something we treasured. However, it snowballed into a large problem for some of my colleagues.

If improperly used, taking a break can turn into, "Hey, has anyone seen Ken this afternoon?" Turns out, Ken's version of taking a break is snoozing in his car for three hours after lunch. Not cool, Ken. Not cool at all. Your boss is the one who decides how long your break can go before you actually need to take a day off.

When taking breaks, especially if you're new to the job, don't take advantage. Instead, use your time wisely and sparingly. After all, you have work to do and that should be your main goal. Remember that you are being judged all the time in the office and if there's a deadline, but you are wasting time sitting outside planning a weekend away with your friends, it will cause unwanted attention. And that attention won't earn you any bonus points.

Tip #7: Elevator Etiquette

What's worse than witnessing bad manners in public? How about bad manners in confined spaces! If you have any sense of claustrophobia, I highly recommend taking the stairs at your new job because the office elevator is like being on a hidden camera TV show where people's wildest quirks come out of the woodwork. From the loud phone talker, to the wacky guy who paces back and forth like he knows something we don't, to the person who carries in a microwaved fish sandwich, you will run into everyone you never wish to meet on the elevator.

When you're on an elevator and the bell rings to let you know it's your floor, why does someone always make a mad dash for the exit like the cables are going to snap? I don't get it. I mean, most elevator doors are motion-censored. Someone just has to put a finger over the door and it won't shut. So why race for the exit? It shows incredibly poor manners to bust through a crowd of people. Even worse is when an elevator rider not only barges through the group, but doesn't even say "Excuse me" as he knocks over women and children without a care.

Another annoying character you'll likely meet on the elevator is the "Mover 'n Shaker." I've had ADHD my entire life and it's something I've been able to manage, but some things do come through. At my desk, I shake my leg like a piston. Annoying, I know. When I'm standing, I move side to side—also annoying. But when I'm on an elevator, I can easily keep things under control. I don't get why some people feel it necessary to pace like Jack Bauer who can't wait to get up to the twentieth floor to dismantle the bomb and rescue everyone. Just keep still for the ten seconds it takes to get to your floor and everyone will have a much smoother ride.

Tip #8: Office Bathroom Etiquette

Using public bathrooms can be a dicey proposition— and that goes double for the workplace. Let's face it, bathrooms are nasty and we don't want to spend any more time in there than we have to. Many people have a phobia of public bathrooms and go out of their way to avoid them, whereas others treat the office bathroom like their own personal retreat.

No matter which side of the coin you fall on, there are four things that will make you the office bathroom pariah:

Toilet Talk

Striking up a conversation with someone while they are in the restroom stall or urinal is an incredible invasion of privacy. For the fellas, we've all had to endure an awkwardness of someone getting chatty and talking over their loud peeing. Ladies have also told me that some people prefer to strike up a chat right outside their bathroom door. How bizarre!

When you do find yourself victim to someone trying to have a casual talk while using the bathroom, simply minimize the conversation potential with a "Mm-hmm . . ." or, "Yup . . ." as a way to let them know you're not interested. Eventually, they'll get the point and slink away.

Target Practice

Similar to awkward bathroom conversations, one of my biggest pet peeves is people who "miss" the toilet, sink, or anything else designed to catch a liquid substance, and then fail to clean up after themselves. When I take my four-year-old daughter to use a public bathroom, I feel like a drill sergeant. "Don't. Touch. Anything!!!!" If she winds up in therapy one day because I treated public bathrooms like poison ivy, then so be it. She'll thank me when she doesn't catch some toxic bacteria.

While at work, I'll use the bathroom throughout the day and inevitably by the late afternoon, I'll find myself standing in a splatter of urine. It's beyond foul! Not only that, when I go to wash my hands, I'll find my shirt sleeves soaked in soapy water that someone else splashed all over the sink. People, a simple wipe of paper towel can cure all of this.

I am by no means telling everyone to be the cleaning crew. But I am saying that when you mess up the seat you should wipe it off. Just a quick swish around the porcelain pony is sufficient. Same for the sink. Use as many paper towels as it takes.

Hand Combat

When people don't wash their hands after using the restroom, I want to rant like I'm making my own gangsta rap album. I can't tell you how many times I've used a restroom and while washing my hands, I see in the mirror someone zip up and walk right out, not even blinking an eye at the sink. I was at the gym one time and saw one guy use the urinal while still wearing his weight-lifting gloves and didn't wash his hands at all. At that point I nearly lost it. (For more on that, see chapter 4.)

Mobile Manners

Like not washing your hands, there's a very fine line between appropriate and "Heck no!" when it comes to using your cell phone in the office bathroom. The line is so thin, it almost disappears when you look closely at it, as was the case with the unmannerly behavior I once witnessed.

I went to the restroom at my office and, while washing my hands, heard loud voices coming from one of the stalls. It turns out, someone was sitting on the toilet and watching what I assumed was an action movie, filled with curse words, screeching cars, and violent shootings. Not that listening to Mozart at full blast while going number two would be any better, but still, this person felt comfortable

"Ugh, can you believe this guy? He wants the
file by noon! Watch this . . . DUH-LETE!"

enough to watch his movie in a workplace stall as if he
was relaxing at home.

In case you're wondering, yes, this *is* disgusting. What
you do in your home is your business, but when you decide
to set up camp at a workplace—or a public—bathroom to
watch a movie or listen to your recent playlist, you are vio-
lating all rules of mannerly behavior. Needless to say, I
didn't stick around to see who the person was or what
happened to the character in the movie who was being
held up at gunpoint.

If you are using the bathroom at work and simply must
use your smartphone as entertainment, don't blast it. In

fact, don't turn up the volume at all. Put your phone on mute. This is not optional.

Tip #9: The First Meeting

After my disastrous first job after college, I was able to escape and found redemption at another company. On my first day there, I went to a meeting with my entire team of thirty people. Being new, and having good manners, I showed up five minutes early. I didn't know anyone so when I got there I introduced myself to people walking in. The room quickly filled up and when the last attendee walked in, she looked at me and said loudly:

"Who is that? Is it 'Bring Your Kid to Work' Day? Whose kid is that? How old is he?"

She said all of this quickly and excitedly and everyone else in the room got very quiet and uncomfortable. Ironically, she was *not* trying to be cruel. This is just how she talks (loud, fast, likes to be heard). After she discovered her error, she was mortified. As an aside, I can't blame her mistake, since at twenty-four I looked all of eighteen. My spiky hair and ill-fitting dress shirt didn't help matters. I very well could have been someone's kid since I was the youngest person on the team by a good twenty years.

Was this an embarrassing way to start a new job?

Definitely!

However, with all the awkwardness of that moment, it actually turned into a great icebreaker and made introducing myself quite easy and memorable. I simply laughed and politely corrected her error. My easy reaction deflated the tension and allowed everyone else to have a chuckle and quickly move on.

There's no denying it—at your first meeting in a new job, you will be on display. But let's say that your first big office meeting does not have the funny misunderstanding that mine did. Let's say your first meeting is, well, *normal*. Your main job at that meeting is to introduce yourself and soak in the office culture and latest business developments. The key is to show that you want to be part of the team.

How do you do that? It all starts from the minute you walk into the room. When you enter, kindly introduce yourself to everyone around you. Shake hands, smile, and kick up a conversation. Be prepared for a very public introduction. Expect your boss to say, "Well, team, today we have a new person joining us . . ." Make sure you have thought of a sentence or two to say to everyone as an introduction. You don't want to be a stuttering, deer-in-the-headlights mess when the spotlight turns on you. Prepare something simple, such as "Hi, I'm [insert name]. I'm excited to meet you all and join the team." Then, during the meeting, sit back, pay attention to the information and the dynamics in the room, and don't interject. You're new and can't possibly have anything of value to add . . . yet. Your job is to learn as much as you can.

> Don't act like you own the place. There's nothing wrong with someone coming in and shaking things up. However, there are still people skills involved in doing so. And if you're the low man on the totem pole, the same rule applies. Proceed with polite caution. Don't assume the bag of Hershey's Kisses in the fridge is free game. People are territorial and nobody likes the new guy shitting in their backyard.
>
> —Benjamin August, screenwriter, producer, and casting director

Tip #10: When to Leave for the Day

So you've survived the first day, attended your first big office meeting and, hopefully, didn't eat the wrong lunch in the refrigerator. Now, it's time to pack up for the day and head home right at 5:00 P.M., right?

WRONG.

So. Very. Wrong.

Even if you have completed your work, even if you spent the entire day hunkered down in your new cube bored to death because there was nothing for you to do, you should still wait to leave with everyone else. If you skip out too early, it shows that you are on your own clock and don't care about the job. Not to say that every single waking thought should be cleared by your boss, but on your first day you need to remember that you have not earned the right to say when you can leave. Plus, how do you know when *is* the right time?

When preparing to leave on your first day, let alone your first week, you should follow the crowd. Watch how your team reacts to the end of the day. Do they all leave at the same time? Do some stay late and some leave early? Why is that? Where do you fit in? You should take particular note of how the office dynamics work towards the end of the day. And no matter what, before you leave on that first day, stop into your boss's office and say good-bye. It's a good idea to stay on your boss's radar and reconnect with him or her to discuss how your first day went. It shows you're a responsible employee. Of course, it doesn't hurt to show the boss that you didn't just bolt out of the office because, hey, "It's five o'clock somewhere."

MODERN MANNERS GUY QUIZ

You just arrived at your new job. You get to your desk and suddenly realize that not only do you have nothing to do, but you don't even know where to start. What's your next move?

Ⓐ Sit back, relax, kick up your feet, and toast your good fortune of landing a job with zero responsibility.

B Holler to your closest colleagues, "CAN SOMEONE TELL ME WHAT THE HELL I'M SUPPOSED TO BE DOING HERE?"

C Settle into your workspace, then walk over to your boss' office, let him/her know you are here, and ask about the details for the day.

D Spend the morning organizing and decorating your desk by printing photos of your friends from your Facebook page on the high-resolution color copier to hang on your walls.

Answer

C When you arrive for your first day, the best thing to do is check in with your boss. If they are not in their office, send an e-mail letting them know you've arrived. If you are not set up on the office e-mail, then use your own. Always make that initial contact. Most of the time, someone will be waiting for you to arrive to show you where you sit, but if you are left alone, don't remain silent. Make yourself known.

MODERN MANNERS GUY'S
FIRST DAY AT WORK TOOL KIT:

1 **HELLO MY NAME IS . . .** Your first day on the job is like meeting the family of the person you've been dating for the past few months—they've heard all about you but you have no idea who they are. So, you will likely have people coming up to you, introducing themselves by the dozen. You will not remember their names. In fact, even if you work in an office of five, you will not remember their names. You'll be too nervous to do so. I recommend having some fun with the situation by wearing a "Hello My Name Is . . ." sticker on your chest. Silly? Perhaps, but it also shows people that you have a sense of humor and is a great icebreaker.

2 **DECORATE YOUR WORKSPACE.** If the "Hello My Name Is . . ." sticker is a bit too out of the box for you, you should still try to make your new workplace comfortable. What better way to show people that you are here to stay—which in turn shows that you are already a member of the team—than decorating your area to make it more personal. Be it books, pictures, even office supplies, if you make your desk look like you are comfortable and happy to be there, it indicates that you're ready to work. Plus, photos are great conversation starters. Of course, you should do any decorating after hours so as not to take time away from your duties.

> **If you go home with somebody, and they don't have books, don't f–k 'em!**
> —John Waters, writer, director, filmmaker

③ BRING BOOKS. My fellow Baltimorean John Waters is right. A bit crude, yes, but still right. I'm not implying that you should necessarily base your choice of partners on the number of books they have. What I am saying is that you shouldn't get involved with someone who doesn't value knowledge. Same thing goes for how you represent yourself at work. If you want people to trust you and your expertise, you should remind them of it on a daily basis. One way to do that is to have plenty of books about your field lining the shelves of your workspace. Not only does this show that you care enough about your job to constantly want to learn more, but it also demonstrates that you are not afraid to look up something if you don't know the answer. And anyway, is there any better decoration than a good book? I think not.

④ ALWAYS CARRY A NOTEPAD. Whenever you go into someone's office or a meeting, you should have a notepad and pen with you; if you're tech savvy, then carry your tablet or laptop. The point is to always have some way to take notes. When you come into a meeting empty-handed, you look unprepared and as if you don't care. On the other hand, if you're always seen taking notes, it shows that you value what others are saying and want to stay on top of things. From day one, you want people to understand that you respect your coworkers and superiors and are willing to learn from them.

5 FIND A BUDDY. On your first day, I highly recommend finding a friendly someone to show you around, help you find things, explain how the office operates, and even go to lunch. You don't want to be the annoying newbie who runs into the boss' office ten times a day with mundane questions like, "Who can I talk to about a parking pass?," "How do I call tech support?," "Where are the cover letters for faxes?" You will inevitably feel lost your first day, but this way at least you can minimize the confusion by asking your new buddy for assistance.

THREE

How to Deal with Annoying Coworkers

The Office Gossip, Cubicle Invaders, and a boatload of other characters you'll want to avoid.

> Never take a "no" from a person who doesn't have the authority to say "yes." You'll meet tons of people who think they know it all but sadly do not. Remember, they are not the end-all and be-all. If you don't get a satisfactory answer from someone, go higher up on the food chain.
> —Helene Parsons, wedding and event planner

I've always considered myself a pretty easy person to get along with. Some would even call me a "people person" because I'm easily able to float in and out of situations and interactions that may rifle others. That's especially true if I'm dealing with the many oddballs I've met throughout my career.

There is a caveat to this: I *choose* when I want to be an extrovert and surround myself with others. If I'm in line at the DMV, you won't see me kicking up a conversation with the lunatic behind me who smells like he hasn't bathed since December 21, 2012, when he thought the Mayan calendar would finally get it right and knock us all out.

However, in a professional setting, you don't always get to choose who you have to work with on a daily basis. No matter where you work, I promise that you'll inevitably find yourself saying, "What planet are they from? And how did they find their way here?"

Handling workplace characters takes time, experience, patience, and a sense of humor. After all, when the Office Weirdo stops you in the hall and talks to you for twenty-five minutes about his rare "Bugs of the Amazon" collection, the only thing you can do (aside from wishing the fire alarm would go off) is laugh.

Laughter is one tool in your arsenal, but over time you'll need to train your body like an endurance athlete to handle the wild characters you'll have to work with, travel with, dine with, or be stuck in the hallway with, unable to escape. And like an endurance athlete, you have to keep your skills sharp for every obstacle that comes your way. Lucky for you, I've dissected some of the most awkward, rude, improper, narcissistic, and downright ignorant types that will make your job feel like the ultimate test of mental composure.

In this chapter, I'll give you examples of some personalities you'll likely encounter in your professional life and how to manage them to your best advantage. You may only have one of these in your office, or you may have them all. Worse still, you may have these, plus another ten to add to my list. But no matter what, after arming yourself with my arsenal of tips, you'll be able to handle anyone who comes your way.

The Pros Weigh In: DAMON YOUNG
Contributing editor at Ebony.com, coauthor of *Your Degrees Won't Keep You Warm at Night,* and founder of VerySmartBrothas.com

• • •

If you ask Damon Young to rattle off some of his accomplishments, you should probably clear your calendar for the rest of the afternoon—it's going to take a while. As an author, columnist, and social satirist, Damon has a keen eye for noticing and illustrating awkward social scenarios that can befall any of us.

I asked Damon how he manages to tolerate the wackiness of others in a professional setting:

> *It's crucial to maintain a level of professionalism whenever you do anything that involves coworkers or work superiors, but there are certain workplaces where a level of informality isn't just accepted, it's expected.*

Whatever your industry, you'll often have to flip the switch from work to play and vice versa. However, Damon says that a professional is a person who can evenly—and effortlessly—balance the way they act around coworkers to be serious, but realistic, and casual, but not out of bounds. A professional remembers that even though they may be doing something deemed "social" they are still under the microscope of their colleagues and superiors.

I played basketball in college, and I still try to play a few times a week. And I can usually watch someone play basketball and tell what kind of person they are. According to people I've worked with, though, I'm a guy who's completely different on the basketball court than I am in the office. At work I'm generally laid back to the point of being near comatose, but I can be rather intense when playing ball, and this has surprised people who only knew me through work.

Damon's example shows how you must balance your personality in the professional world versus the one that emerges in your personal/off-hours world. If you are the "intense basketball player" on and off the court, and you work in an accounting firm, no one will want to associate with you. You have to be able to balance your recreational—or off-hours—personality with the one you bring into the boardroom. There is a need for intensity, but not all the time. In the same way, being laid back 24/7 will make you appear lazy or unenthusiastic. Knowing that you can be aggressive (or calm) when needed is a strong quality to keep in your back pocket. And don't be afraid to use it.

> You don't want to come across as too pushy or
> too over the top or too quiet. It is best to be like a
> politician early on. Come in moderate and get the
> lay of the land. You need to be adaptable and flexible
> as you move through the organization and be aware of which
> groups you are working with and how they interact.
>
> —Brooks Dame, CEO of Proof Eyewear

Modern Manners Guy's Top 10 Tips for Handling Annoying Coworkers

Annoying Coworker #1: Mr./Ms. Know-It-All

I get it—you went to a *very* nice school.

And yes, you have been here longer than anyone.

And I know you have seen it all *and* done it all and you know what's best.

Meet Mr. or Ms. Know-It-All. This person will stop at nothing to tell you exactly how right they are/were/will be on any topic. He or she has delusions of grandeur. If you went rock climbing over the weekend, he climbed Mt. Kilimanjaro. If you got tickets to the big game, he once got to sit on the sideline and even call a play or two.

And that great job you did on the big presentation? Well, she can do (and has done) it much, much better.

I've worked with a Mr. Know-It-All. After he found out that I was a professional wrestler for eight years (no kidding!), he claimed that he paid his way through college as a cage fighter . . . back in the early 1990s . . . when cage fighting wasn't even on TV, let alone something at which you could make money like you can today. Plus, a quick Web search of his name brought up nothing. I should not have been surprised. This was the same guy who was one cut away from making an NFL team's open tryouts, five years after graduating college. At 5'7" and a slim-and-trim 400 pounds, this guy couldn't last five minutes *standing* in line for NFL tryouts, let alone come anywhere close to making the team. So you could understand my reluctance to believe his claims. But here was a person who knew it all, saw it all, and could top anything you did a million times over.

Here's the bottom line on Mr. and Ms. Know-It-All: They're full of shit.

Everyone in the office knows this person is a compulsive liar, yet we all have to deal with them. Inevitably, at some point you will want to ring their Know-It-All neck. But since we're all professionals and would rather not go to jail, you tolerate this person to the best of your ability. But how do you work with someone who is so irrational?

For starters, prepare your facts. If you have to work together on a project, have your part ready, airtight, with no holes and make sure to have supporting documents to uphold your ideas.

Secondly, don't get riled up. Unfortunately, the Know-

It-All will not suddenly realize that their proclamations of success are ridiculous. So if you know you are right, and everyone else does, too, just nod and smile at their outrageous claim of holding the Guinness World Record for most ice cream cones eaten in ten minutes. If you try to engage, you will just rile them up and make it worse for yourself. Instead, just let it roll off you like water off a duck's back.

On the flip side, if the Know-It-All stakes a claim on your idea or your work, you have the right to stand up to them. Know-It-Alls are bullies (I'll touch more on that in a bit) and when it matters, you have to stand up to a bully or you will get walked over.

For example, let's say the Know-It-All takes credit for your work on a project. Ask them (preferably in front of others) when, how, and what their results were. Ask pointed questions about specific details that only the creator of the work (aka, you) would know the answer to. Chances are, the Know-It-All will crumble and retreat to lies that you can't debunk so easily—like how they once played backup guitar for Lady Gaga before she made it big. Riiight.

Annoying Coworker #2: The MVP

> It is amazing what you can accomplish
> if you do not care who gets the credit.
> —Harry S. Truman, 33rd president of the United States

In a team environment, this is the attitude you should have. However, not everyone does. This brings me to the close cousin of the Know-It-All: the Office MVP. Similar in many ways, but drastically different in the core values of what makes them tick.

Whereas the Know-It-All knows it all and will tell you so, the Office MVP may not be as bold or flashy with their accomplishments. But don't let that fool you. The Office MVP *is* very accomplished—because they take credit for everyone else's work and just so happen to be around when the kudos are given out by the boss. The Office MVP doesn't necessarily have to be a major player on the team or a part of the project/meeting that got all the praise from the CEO, yet that won't stop them from taking credit for other people's success.

When dealing with the Office MVP, the key is to out-think them. You have to anticipate that they will always be around waiting to pounce on you and your hard work like a lion stalking an innocent antelope in the Serengeti. But unlike the kind, gentle antelope who gets trapped by the lion and eaten alive, you have the ability to escape the MVP's clutches by working around them.

For starters, outline and nail down the specific roles of each player on your team. John does the scheduling, Tim does the calls, Rachel does the research, etc. It doesn't matter how many people you have either, just as long as everyone is clear on their duties. If you aren't, call a meeting with your team or boss to ensure the goals and progress are on track.

Track your conversations to the team in e-mails and meetings. Keep copies of key communication. That way, when the kudos are given out and all of a sudden your core team of six people has become seven, you are able to politely show that the real credit is due only to the original six.

Just because the MVP attended one meeting, or was copied on one e-mail, does not mean that he was an essential cog in the machine. Use the leverage you've acquired throughout the project process to support your success. In the business world, people will often try to take credit for your work and it's up to you to stand up for yourself with concrete supporting evidence. Once you do this, the Office MVP will realize you can't be messed with and instead of going after you, will chase down easier prey.

Annoying Coworker #3: The Bully

Forget what you know about bullies. The Bully is not the kind of bully you dealt with in school who was physically intimidating and took pride in humiliating you in front of your classmates.

In the workplace, The Bully will likely not be a ripped jock or an angry meathead who uses his muscles to make a point. Instead, The Bully is someone who has some form of authority and uses that as a weapon against others. In my opinion, The Bully is the worst of all the unmannerly characters you will meet at work because they're often not easy to avoid and could be a key player in how you are perceived by upper management. And of course, The Bully could also be your boss.

Think about Kevin Spacey's character in the film *Horrible Bosses*. He epitomized the slick jerk. There's also Darth Vader, who would literally chop off your head for screwing up. But my all-time favorite is Bill Lumbergh in *Office Space*, who has become a cult classic villain. I'll never forget his famous line, "I'm gonna need you to go ahead and come in tomorrow . . . Oh, and I almost forgot, I'm also gonna need you to go ahead and come in on Sunday too, m'kay?"

It gives me chills just thinking about his droning voice.

These are just a few classic examples of bullies who took advantage of their power with ruthless aggression. And despite these being fictional characters, there are absolute truths that make these characters relatable in real life.

In my often-cited, miserable first job after college, I dealt with a Bully who happened to be my boss. In typical bully fashion, he was nice one minute and then threw me under the bus the next, depending on what was necessary to make himself look good. Then the cycle would repeat itself. And like many others in my predicament, I was trapped—or rather, I *felt* trapped—because I was inexperienced and thought this was how things were done.

I was wrong.

And like all the people in the movies who were picked on by bullies, I hit a breaking point when I decided enough was enough. And deciding you will not take it anymore is the first step in handling a bully.

Bullies are only as powerful as the myths that are created around them (except for Darth Vader—that guy was a legit sociopath). These myths—usually created by other employees or past associates—give bullies greater power and make them into bigger, badder monsters than they really are. Sadly, many of the myths surrounding my Office Bully were actually true. He was mean, conniving, a thief, a compulsive liar, and enjoyed putting people down in front of others.

The Bully preys on the weak, so if you are approached by The Bully with some task he wants to unload on you, say no from the beginning and stand your ground.

I know what you're thinking: "This person has been here forever, they're senior to me. Who am I to say no?"

You, my dear friend, are a human being with a backbone. Act like it.

Take this very common situation. The Bully comes to you and says, "Ken, take these papers to the copier for me. I have a lot of work to do." So Ken, being the new guy, does it unquestioningly. Ken wants to be a team player but The Bully is taking advantage of him. Ken now becomes The Bully's errand boy. Is that why you spent $50,000 a year for college? To be someone's errand runner? I don't think so.

What Ken should say is, "Sorry, but I can't do that right now. I'm working on a project that has a strict deadline. I'd be happy to help you another time."

Then the interaction is complete. Don't continue to apologize. Don't drag it on. Just end it politely and walk away. You are not being unhelpful or impolite. You are simply stating a fact that he or she can't possibly argue with.

If he had said, "I'm really jammed for this meeting and have to make copies. I know you're busy, but would you mind giving me a hand?" then it would be another story. Expressing compassion for your time followed by a genuine request for help would actually deserve your help.

However, The Bully is usually just lazy and looking to take advantage of you. Watch out!

Annoying Coworker #4: The Cubicle Invader

How many times have you found yourself waiting in line and someone is standing so close to you, it feels like you're already in an intimate relationship with them? The Line Crowder is incredibly annoying and quick to invade your space and breathe down your neck without a care in the world.

Unfortunately, there is usually one of these in every office—except that at work, this character is known as the Cubicle Invader. His mission is to invade your personal space at all costs. He or she usually finds you at your desk, where you have nowhere to hide. The Cubicle Invader comes in many forms—all of which make you want to wave the white flag and surrender.

They often prefer the old "just popping in" routine. You are hard at work and then like a crash of thunder on a sunny day, they bust into your space and start chatting about . . . something. If they don't crash into the spare seat next to you, they find complete comfort in draping their arms over the narrow opening of your cubicle, blocking you from the outside world—*freedom*!

When this happens, you have to think like an NFL coach—the best offense is a sound defense. If you hear the Cubicle Invader approaching, make your area unwelcoming. Place your purse, your briefcase, your jacket, or stack of papers on the extra chair or on the available space on your desk, so they can't park on it for hours. If you don't barricade yourself in time and the Cubicle Invader makes landfall, you can mention that you have to take a call in a few minutes and when that "time" comes, hop on the phone, dismissing them with a smile and mouthing, "I'll catch up with you later." Granted, these may not be the nicest ways to get rid of somebody, but in times of desperation, it's every man and woman for themselves.

"Man, oh man, I've been here for like an hour! We should go get lunch soon. But first, did I ever tell you about the time in college when I led my fraternity to the flag football championship?"

The Pros Weigh In: BROOKS DAME
CEO of Proof Eyewear

• • •

Brooks Dame is a humble guy from Eagle, Idaho, who grew up working in his family's lumber business. Years ago, Brooks created a pair of sunglasses made out of sustainable wood and showed them off to some friends. Word got around and next thing he knew, his role in the family business became drastically different. He recruited his younger brothers and Proof Eyewear was born.

Brooks will say that no two pieces of wood are the same, and since Proof Eyewear products are made from wood, no two pairs of sunglasses are the same. It's also a philosophy that Brooks follows when dealing with people. Some people will be easy for you to get along with, but many will not.

You're not always going to agree with colleagues. That's just the way it is. And disagreeing is OK. It sometimes creates conversation. We've not always agreed on which products to roll out, which ways to market our products, how to get funding, etc. For me the best thing to do when I'm not on the same page with a coworker or group is to first make sure they can support their point with facts and ideas. If they can't and are just disagreeing to disagree or play devil's advocate, they usually either convince me or realize that their position isn't a good one.

The other thing I do is sometimes walk away from the argument. This allows me to clear my head on the point of contention, do more research, create valid points to strengthen my position, or look at other options. Sometimes taking a break gets both myself and the other party to remove the tension and talk substance. I always like to say, "We aren't curing cancer here, we make sunglasses."

I recommend taking some time and thinking through big decisions. There's no reason to force something or agree to something if you aren't comfortable. This isn't to say you can sit on the sidelines forever, but sometimes taking a step back and looking at the issue from a different angle can help you make some meaningful discoveries.

Annoying Coworker #5: The Gossip

Of the most annoying workplace characters you're likely to encounter, none is more annoying than The Gossip. This person knows everything about everyone and makes it their mission to share the wealth with whoever will listen. You may not have even asked, but I promise you will find out more than you ever wished to know about the intrigues of company life. "So the new guy in accounting, I hear he's dating Michelle from HR. You didn't hear this from me, though." My favorite is the "Between me and you . . ." The "Between me and you" is The Gossip's calling card. This person opens with that to whet your appetite and then lay down some awful news like, "I heard that Ken is getting fired tomorrow." The Gossip lives in a world of lies and distorted truths, and wants you to join in the scandal.

Like The Bully, The Gossip comes in many forms. It's not always the perky extrovert who wants to know everyone's business. In fact, The Gossip is a chameleon that takes the form of whatever situation they are in and like the sneaky little reptile, they are always waiting in the corner for someone to fall into their trap. The Gossip is usually friendly, enjoys talking to others, and loves being a part of the team . . . but only because they crave attention and need more fuel for their rumor-mongering habit.

What seems like a casual trip down the street to get coffee with The Gossip can turn into a Barbara Walters special on the Ten Most Fascinating People in the Office. Let's say while you're getting coffee, the Gossip tells you excitedly that Carol in marketing is padding her expense reports because she maxed out her credit card. You had no idea and didn't want this information, but now you know. You're trapped and have become an accomplice in the scheme. Put it this way: you may not have robbed the bank, but if you knew it was going to happen and did nothing about it, you are still guilty.

So when The Gossip unethically shares confidential or personal information about your coworkers, you are complicit. Let's now say that because The Gossip likes to spread news around to anyone who will listen, rumors of Carol's indiscretions find their way to the vice president of accounting. Then the question arises, "Who knew about this?" Well, unfortunately, because of your coffee break, you did—and The Gossip would have no qualms about throwing you under the bus. Now what do you do?

Gossip in the office is never a good idea. It makes people nervous to have information they shouldn't. The best way to stay out of The Gossip's web is to avoid it altogether. If you're in a group setting and you see a wave of gossip coming on, busy yourself with something like "an important phone call" and step away from the conversation.

If The Gossip catches you in the hall and stops to chat, find an excuse to leave as soon as the conversation takes a turn for the improper. "Hey, that sounds good but I have to run to a meeting. You around later? We'll catch up." At work, this is a perfectly acceptable way to dodge a bad conversation.

The other thing you can do if dodging isn't an option is to simply change the topic. When you see it going down a bad road, bring up something new—something totally innocent and gossip-free, like the weather—and don't let it go back to the gossip. Do this just until you can escape. After you are gone, The Gossip can find someone else to parlay their poison. Someone who hasn't read this book.

Annoying Coworker #6: The Loud Talker

Last week, Shawn and Gretchen broke up. Gretchen begged Shawn not to leave her but Shawn, who is from Connecticut but went to school in Florida and who works on Wall Street trading energy stocks, well, he's decided to move on.

I learned about this only because Gretchen has chatted with and cried for Shawn every day—over the phone, at work—for the past two months.

"And he still won't commit! What is he thinking?"

I get that you might have to have personal phone conversations during the workday, but just remember that your sneeze can often be heard rows away. Never mind that screaming phone brawl Gretchen and Shawn were having last Tuesday.

If you don't have an office door you can close, try to take your personal calls into a more private area, like the coffee shop downstairs, the stairwell, or a nearby park.

If you're the one forced to listen to a coworker yelling, crying, or loudly telling her best friend about the new person she's seeing or the new antidepressant her doctor just prescribed that's giving her hives in unexpected places, you need to nip this in the bud quickly. I recommend this not just because The Loud Talker can affect your productivity, but they can also affect your reputation as well. If you're on a business call and the person on the other end can hear Gretchen weeping about being on a break with Shawn, that's never good for business.

For this situation, there is only one answer. You need to take Gretchen aside and let her know that she is speaking way too loudly and becoming an embarrassment. If it takes you having to be her shoulder to cry on for the moment, do it for the sake of your fellow coworkers. They'll appreciate it. Plus, someone had to tell Gretchen that Shawn has also been seeing Abby in marketing for the past three weeks anyway. That's courtesy of Michelle, The Gossip.

Annoying Coworker #7: The Stud

In the 1980s, when dinosaurs roamed the earth, ZZ Top sang, "Every girl's crazy 'bout a sharp-dressed man."

In the 1990s Right Said Fred told us, "I'm too sexy for my shirt, so sexy it hurts." Then, in 2006, Justin Timberlake brought "SexyBack."

I myself was missing sexy and am just happy it returned—and so is The Stud. He's the one sexy hangs out with. They go for drinks every night. When The Stud walks into the room, he moves in slow motion, with the wind flowing through his slick hair and paparazzi snapping photos; women get light-headed, their knees buckling.

It's important to understand that the Stud isn't necessarily the gorgeous person you're envisioning. No, my friends, The Stud *thinks* that he could give George Clooney charm lessons and wipe the floor with Brad Pitt. The reality is often very different. Sure, he may get lucky from time to time— usually by picking up some poor victim in a bar at 2:00 A.M. who has spent the past six hours drowning her sorrows in shots of tequila—but even if he strikes out on a daily basis, his game in the office is always set to 11.

The Stud's misguided, overly sex-charged, hormonal fourteen-year-old behavior causes a lot of friction (and not the fun kind) with other people in the office. There's a little thing I like to call "Sexual Harassment" that The Stud does not seem to believe in. "Come on, I'm just playing around! I didn't mean anything. Where's your sense of humor?" This will be his response when you mention that asking the intern in the miniskirt to pick up papers off the floor isn't exactly kosher.

Often people feel that there is no defense against The Stud because his overly confident exterior is impermeable. There's no way you could break their spirit. This is entirely incorrect. The Stud is actually an insecure ball of mush, surrounded by a thin layer of bravado. One quick, witty jab to his ego and he'll collapse like the stack of *Playboy*s on his dresser.

Take my coworker Dave, for example. During a lunch outing with four other employees, Dave kept "jokingly" asking the new intern about what she would be wearing to the office holiday party later that weekend. When she replied with simply "a dress," The Stud wasn't satisfied. He prodded further, wondering if it was short, tight, low-cut. She ignored him until finally she said, "Well, what are *you* wearing?" The Stud was intrigued. "A casual suit," he said.

Then she asked, "What about your date? What will she be wearing?" But before The Stud could reply, the intern took out a glove from her jacket pocket, tossed it on the table and said, "This is probably what your little date will be wearing." The whole table erupted with laughter and Dave turned fifty shades of purple from embarrassment. You won't be surprised to learn that he never picked on the intern again.

Annoying Coworker #8: The Best Friend

Annoying coworkers are about as common as annoying meetings, and no matter where you work, there's always going to be someone who could very well qualify for the title of Most Annoying Person Who Ever Existed. But because you are so cool, charming, and generally awesome, this person has decided you are their new best friend, their BFF, their amigo, a member of their wolf pack. Lucky you!

This character is known as The Best Friend and he or she will latch onto you like a twelve-year-old girl to a life-sized Justin Bieber cutout. This person will follow you to the copy machine, ask if you want to get coffee, e-mail you pictures or funny articles that A) aren't funny and B) have nothing to do with work, and of course, they'll invite you to lunch every day. Every. Single. Day. And don't you dare try to make plans with someone else! Your new best friend has already booked you for the next five years.

Unlike real best friends, the office Best Friend will cause you more misery than happiness. Of course, it's nice to have someone pay attention to you, but not if that attention comes from someone who just doesn't get the hint. If you are the one who attracts said annoying coworker, then I'm very sorry for you. But have no fear, there is light at the end of the tunnel . . . just don't turn around because chances are that annoying coworker followed you into the tunnel.

So is there a nice way of saying "I'm just not that into you" to a colleague?

Well, because this is your workplace, you have to be careful about how you deal with the unwanted Best

Friend. You can't be as stern as you may be with someone in your personal life because you see this person every day and, honestly, may even end up working directly with or even *for* them at some point. So you don't want to burn any bridges. That's why flat-out telling this person to leave you alone is not an option. That leaves you with two possibilities:

1. **Reject their advances.** If they ask you to lunch, always politely decline. Drinks after work? Nope, can't make it. Carpool to the conference? No, I'm driving with someone already. This way, you're making yourself very clear without being blunt. For this strategy to work you must be consistent. Do not accept lunch (even if they're buying); do not follow your rejection of the carpool with "Would you like to join us?" Mixed messages will only prolong the unwanted attention.

2. **Talk to the boss.** If a person is constantly smothering you at work, you can easily tell your boss. However, don't say, "Bob is always around me and won't leave me alone!" That's just complaining. Try something like, "I'm sure Bob is a great guy, but he is spending way too much time by my desk and honestly it's distracting me from my duties." If you position the attention as something that reduces your productivity, your boss will jump to handle it. And you can even request that your name be kept out of the conversation.

Annoying Coworker #9: The E-mail Ranter

> There are different rules for reading, for thinking, and for talking. Writing blends all three of them.
> —Dr. Mason Cooley, American aphorist

I love this quote, and not just because I'm a writer, but because it describes how powerful something you write can be for those who read it.

I'm pretty sure that Dr. Cooley was not talking about e-mail, but it can certainly apply. Nowadays, people take the power of words for granted. Whenever they hop behind their computers, they become the most influential, powerful, humorous, and creative minds to ever grace the Internet. That is also the case at work where people like to flex their e-mail muscles on everything from politics and sports to why there is not enough variety of salad dressings in the cafeteria. Why is it that when some people get behind that keyboard, they become more unmannerly with every exclamation point and emoticon?

Whether you call it "witty," "brave," or just "opinionated," writing nasty things in e-mail about other people is actually called bullying (see Annoying Coworker #3). And in the office, e-mail bullying has a ripple effect. The E-mail Ranter is very quick to post comments or send e-mails that are so offensive and harsh, that in a million years they wouldn't have the guts to say them in person. And if confronted, The E-mail Ranter will most likely act as if nothing wrong was done.

A perfect example of The E-mail Ranter became national news in 2012 when TV newswoman Jennifer Livingston received a letter from a viewer who wrote that she was unfit to be on TV because of her weight. The newswoman stood up for herself, publicly pointing out how rude this guy was and posting his e-mail rant online, along with his name. I gave her a standing ovation. Predictably, the bully who sent the e-mail backed off and apologized immediately. What did he think would happen? That the newswoman would thank him for his astute commentary? That she would retire? It was not helpful, it was rude, and like most E-mail Ranters, this guy did not have the guts to say his piece in person.

It's rude—and cowardly—to call someone names. We all learned this in kindergarten. Heck, my four-year-old knows not to call people names! But behind a keyboard, well, everyone is hilarious and brave, right? Wrong! You are a fool if you think that posting rude statements in an e-mail makes you cool—and even more of a fool if you think your employers aren't reading your e-mails. (They are. Definitely.)

Next time you get an e-mail from someone ranting about something or someone in the office, just click delete. If the e-mail is directed at you, then I suggest approaching them in person. Don't get confrontational; simply ask what the goal is of their rudeness. I promise you, they will quickly morph into a coward. I do this all the time at work. When a colleague e-mails me something insulting, I simply walk over, sit down in their office or cube, and ask what's up. They immediately act like it was no big deal and that we are the best of friends.

Bottom line: E-mail Ranters are wimps disguised as overconfident imbeciles. What appears as intelligence is really ignorance. E-mailing something hate-filled is about as courageous as the guy who sits in his house cursing at the NFL quarterback over a bad throw, saying he could have made that 85-yard touchdown pass with his eyes closed.

Annoying Coworker #10: Mr./Ms. Do You Know Who I Am?

Who doesn't love to see a spoiled rich kid who, after taking six years to get through college, walks right into dad's company, past the guy who has been there for ten years, past the woman who has been there since the company began, and finds a nice cozy corner office waiting for them? I for one love when this happens! Who doesn't love Mr. and Ms. Do You Know Who I Am? We see them on every single celebrity reality show where someone is famous because their parents did something cool. Or the ones who think they are corporate giants because their grandparents founded a company a half century ago, which they had the genetic luck to fall into.

All joking aside, I loathe this person. They're the reason why anyone with the last name Kardashian is famous (well, that and a well-timed sex tape).

We'd all like to think that people get ahead based on their smarts, their skills, and their dedication. That's mostly true. However, in your professional career you will undoubtedly run into a situation where someone has a plum position and countless perks simply because they knew (or are related to) someone at the top. Mr. or Ms. Do You Know Who I Am? feels entitled to a certain level of authority in the office and has no remorse about flexing their arrogance. Unfortunately, you will not be able to avoid them.

The ego of this privileged person will affect your work. It's just inevitable. But *how* they affect your work is up to you. If you pay close attention to their triggers and soft spots, you can use that information to make your life easier.

I'm sure you've seen this scenario in a movie or TV show: Some hotshot celebrity or rich guy goes into a restaurant and tries to pull rank by telling the hostess, "Do you know who I am?" Then the manager comes running up to calm the scene and take the VIP (Very Ignorant and Pompous) customer to their seat. It's a classic scene and when I first heard it in the workplace, I had to chuckle. I mean, who really says that? Who honestly thinks—out loud, mind you—that people should know who they are at all times. Some call it a difference between the haves and have-nots but if being rude to everyone around you makes you a "haver" than I'm happy to be one of the nots.

Along with the obvious difference in bank accounts, the main difference between you and Mr./Ms. Do You Know Who I Am? is that it will take a major corporate overthrow to get rid of them, whereas you can be fired at any time, without warning. And knowing that is key in working with Mr./Ms. Do You Know Who I Am?.

Mr./Ms. Do You Know Who I Am? come in a few different forms, all of which can be properly managed by simply appeasing their egos while at the same time creatively working around their limitations. Like in any other relationship, you'll have to make a connection with Mr./Ms. Do You Know Who I Am?; however, this connection is not necessarily a two-way street. You will have to make the effort and you will have to find their triggers. Once you do, you can build bridges where there were serious gaps in communication, simply because you and this person see eye to eye on something of interest to them.

Let me be clear: Mr./Ms. Do You Know Who I Am? are not always ill-intentioned people. Some of these fortunate individuals do actually want to work and even make the company better. Unfortunately, ego often gets in the way of even the kindest Mr./Ms. Do You Know Who I Am?. So let's take at look at three types of Mr./Ms. Do You Know Who I Am? and ways to manage working with them:

This is the top tier of the Mr./Ms. Do You Know Who I Am? ladder. The one who gave the writers of *Gossip Girl* more than enough material for their spoiled-brat characters. For starters, this person never really had to try for anything in their life. They skated their way through high school, drank their way through college, and took the express lane to the corner office where they spend all day surfing the Web to find the best vacation spot to try out that weekend. This person isn't always rude, some may be very pleasant, but they generally lack any drive whatsoever. That's not a crime. But it is a huge hurdle to get over when it comes time for you to work with them.

When dealing with this type of colleague, you have to make peace with the fact that they will not be fired, demoted, or reprimanded. You are at the mercy of their ignorance to their responsibilities and you will have to thoroughly reinforce what needs to be done, without pissing them off in the process. For this, I recommend finding a common interest or connection. For example, let's say your Mr. Do You Know Who I Am? loves cars. Whether you share this passion or not is irrelevant; you should still use this info to form a connection. Simply go to a car Web site and see what the latest and greatest thing is. Take that info and forward them a message like, "I'm sure you've already seen that Maserati just released a sneak peek at next year's model. Can you believe the horsepower on this thing?" This is not sucking up—it's making a connection that is necessary to get work done. The more they see you as someone with similar interests, the more eager they will be to work with you and move things along when needed (or at least step aside and get out of the way to let others get the job done).

#2: The Driven Scion

Unlike in the above example where Mr./Ms. Do You Know Who I Am? feel that their name or position in life is all they need to get by, some people of good fortune actually . . . wait for it . . . want to work! What? Get out of here! You're talking crazy!

All joking aside, yes my friends, you will—if you're lucky—run into an eager young person who wants to do more than just raid the company coffers to buy themselves an island. This person is a valued asset because they're driven to succeed at their job (whether that's because they want to make a name for themselves or because they actually had work ethic built into their DNA). This form of Mr./Ms. Do You Know Who I Am? may have used that title before but it probably wasn't their proudest moment.

Similar to example #1, the key to working well with this type of Mr./Ms. Do You Know Who I Am? is to build on a common interest, but using a much more professional approach. When you bring up a topic, make it more work-related than leisure. You may get the chance to talk about leisure during off hours, but this person needs to see you as someone who thinks about business before pleasure.

For example, the driven Ms. Do You Know Who I Am? I worked with was very tech savvy, so I made sure to connect with her on geeky subjects. From time to time I would e-mail an article from a leading news source highlighting something that would benefit the company. Maybe it was new software we could implement or a new analytics program we should look into, but in every situation I wanted her to know that I could see her vision for the company and work with it. It worked!

#3: The "I'm Just One of You . . . Sometimes"

In all these situations the people who throw around the title of Mr./Ms. Do You Know Who I Am? are there for reasons that may not be based on their own merits. But there are instances when you come across someone who is not only driven, but also knows the plight of the everyman. Sure their office is much bigger, their pockets a heck of a lot deeper, and they can fly off to places for the weekend that would cost you a year's salary, but those are perks that anyone in their position would take. I would! Admit it, you would, too.

This person may have the luxuries of the Heir/Heiress, but isn't showy about it. They may have the drive of the Scion but are less anal and able to relax sometimes. There is less of a wall with this form of Mr./Ms. Do You Know

Who I Am? and that is your "in." You should connect with this type on multiple levels, personal and professional, unlike the other two examples. They tend to be more open-minded and you can feel more comfortable voicing dissenting opinions without getting booted. The door to their office may be more open than the others. In fact, when you have someone who has worked their way up from the mailroom to the boardroom, you actually want them to throw around the Do You Know Who I Am? because they are generally doing it to push an important issue involving the company and not just to get a nice table at some fancy restaurant.

MODERN MANNERS GUY QUIZ

A fellow coworker is constantly coming over to your desk to talk to you for long periods of time. You don't like talking to them, but they plant themselves in your space for ages to complain about their dating life or other non-work-related issues. What do you do?

Ⓐ Whenever you hear them approaching, fake a phone call and gesture apologetically that you can't talk now.

Ⓑ Ask them if they don't mind coming back another time, or maybe catch up at lunch, because you have deadlines to get to before the end of the day.

C Stop what you're doing and give them your undivided attention. The debate over who made a better Batman, Michael Keaton or Christian Bale, is an important topic for discussion.

D Take a forty-five-minute coffee break at 9:00 a.m. to hear about their cousin's best friend's fiancé who they are convinced is cheating.

Answer

B Let me first say that there's nothing wrong with talking casually with a coworker about things outside of work. Allowing coworkers to be open and friendly with one another is ideal for building a unified team and for boosting morale. However (and this is a big however), there is a time and place for everything. Chatting for ten minutes about last night's nail-biter football game is fine, but squatting at someone's desk for an hour to discuss the movie version of *50 Shades of Grey* is not.

If you find yourself stuck in this whirlpool of annoying chatter, you have to get out before they drag you under with them. Yes, you can be a shoulder to lean on, and someone they should feel open to talk to, but your desk is not the place for it. Let the person know when they walk in (since you know why they are coming over) that you have a call to get to in five minutes. Even if you don't, make one up. I don't generally advocate lying but I do advocate not hurting someone's feelings. If your evasive action doesn't get the point across, it's time to lay down the cold hard truth. Say simply that you have too much on your plate and deadlines are looming and you simply don't have time to talk. Don't be harsh, just honest. Let that person know that you are available to talk away from your desk, off hours or at lunch, because you prefer not to have people around you hear private conversations.

MODERN MANNERS GUY'S IMPROPER COWORKERS TOOL KIT

1 **HEADPHONES ARE LIFESAVERS.** Being in an office environment, headphones could very well be the greatest weapon you have against annoyances around you. The person next to you talking too loud? Pop in your headphones. Someone blaring "Call Me Maybe" on infinite repeat? Headphones. Headphones allow you to tune out everyone around you by tuning into something you enjoy. Keep a pair at your desk at all times. These are your office headphones, not to be taken home with you. Trust me, you will go nuts when you realize that you accidentally left them at home and are now stuck having to listen to your neighbor crying on the phone to her therapist about why she got dumped.

2 **PHOTOS OF YOUR SPECIAL SOMEONE.** Having photos of friends and family at your desk can be a great way to show you are comfortable in your new workplace. Plus, posting a photo of your significant other on your desk will help keep The Stud away from you. Generally, once The Stud knows you are off limits, they will leave you alone or at least tone down the studliness to manageable levels.

③ POST FUNNY CARTOONS ON YOUR WALL. The creators of *The Far Side*, *Working Daze*, and *Dilbert* had a real insight into office culture. They were able to shed light on the bizarre and inappropriate behaviors of cubicle dwellers. And these comics can be a great way to point out something in your office that is bothering you that you don't feel comfortable saying out loud. Don't pick one that is offensive—you don't want to be rude—but you can be witty. For example, find a cartoon that uses a safe character like an animal or even a caveman (*Far Side* used this technique amazingly well) that illustrates the situation at hand. Do not choose a drawing with a person who resembles the frequent offender. This way, you're only hinting at a certain someone without shoving their nose in it. But anyone who sees the picture will think, "Oh, I get it, that's Brian."

④ THE ART OF BODY LANGUAGE. You can say a lot without saying a word and this is a key tool in the workplace. For example, if you walk over to me and I shake my head without saying a word, you know I can't be bothered. Or if I hold up one index finger and tilt my head toward the computer, you know I can't talk right now because I'm on deadline. To show that you are too busy to chat (especially when The Gossip is nearby), turn your chair around so that the back is facing the opening of your cubicle or office door and place a lot of papers and charts on the desk in front of you. When your back is visible, people are less likely to bother you. If they don't get the not-so-subtle hint and come in anyway, simply turn around, roll your eyes, and lift a stack of paper in your hand. This will let them know that of course you would rather talk to them but can't because of all this work you're stuck doing.

FOUR

Socializing at Work

Meet your new social circle—whether you like it
or not.

> It's always annoying when a business professional sends an
> auto DM [direct message] on Twitter. Nothing says personal
> like a canned response offering me your free e-book.
> —Tim McDonald, community manager at Huffington Post Live

Your colleagues are a lot like your extended family—
except that you spend much more time with your
coworkers than you do with your relatives. So inevitably, they wind up being a large part of your social
circle. Some of my closest friends are people I met at work.
One guy I met at a job served as a groomsman at my wedding. We became friends the same way we all do as kids,
by randomly being thrown into a situation together and
hitting it off. However, not all offices are welcoming places
where you will fall head over heels for your colleagues. In
fact, it is likely that at some point in your career you will

be at a job where you have to patiently tolerate your co-workers until 5:00 P.M. strikes.

The thing to remember is that no matter how hard you work or how smart you are, it's the relationships you build in your job that will either forward or tank your career.

Socializing at work takes many forms, from dining with colleagues and superiors, to sharing a workstation, to holiday gatherings, and even exercising in the company gym. Having worked in large corporations and in small companies, I've had the chance to witness the different dynamics of workplace social interaction on both sides of the spectrum. But the one similarity is that whether you work in an office of six or a conglomerate of 6,000, you will inevitably be drawn to someone or a group of people who share your opinions, values, and sense of humor. The tricky bit is that you won't always get to work with them. You may have to work with people with whom you have zilch in common. And you will have to make the best of it.

So before you walk into the office for the day, take a good hard look around you and ask yourself this question: How much do I really want to be around these people?

If your answer is "I can see my coworkers becoming real friends" then you are well on your way to properly handling anything that comes your way since you have that comfortable group to lean on. However, if your answer is, "Someone save me!" well, in that case, you have an uphill battle ahead of you. But have no fear, with a little reality check and a willingness to develop your social skills, you can have a much more productive professional life (even if your colleagues are trolls).

The Pros Weigh In: CHRISTA FOLEY
Senior HR manager at Zappos.com, Inc.

• • •

Every year, *Fortune* magazine releases its list of the Top 100 Companies to Work For, which grant the lucky 100 the ultimate bragging rights. One company that has found itself in the top tier of *Fortune*'s list time and time again is online shoe retailer Zappos.

Zappos is writing the book on happiness in the workplace. No, really, CEO Tony Hsieh actually wrote a book called *Delivering Happiness: A Path to Profits, Passion, and Purpose* that has garnered a cult-like following and illustrates that a healthy and happy work environment is key to creating a highly productive (and profitable) company. When I reached out to Tony, he suggested I talk to one of his top employees, Christa Foley. As the senior HR manager for Zappos Christa's main job it is to ensure that employee happiness stays intact.

In fact, not only is building a happy work environment key for Zappos' success, but the company's focus is to hire employees who truly want to be there and become part of a family. How committed is Christa and her team to only hiring people who feel passionate about what they do? How about by offering a no-questions-asked check for

$2,000 to leave during their initial four-week training period? Seriously, $2,000—to quit! This has to be a crazy idea, right? That's what Christa thought, too:

> *When Tony first came to us with this idea, we thought, "Everyone's going to take the offer. Everyone's going to quit!" But it hasn't been that way. The training is four weeks and this [offer] happens on the second week. The original concept started because we didn't want people to stay here just for the paycheck. It's $2,000 and people are given the opportunity to think about it and see if they want to A) stay with us or B) go somewhere else. If working at Zappos is not something they're passionate about, we want to know that right away.*

I know what you're wondering: How many people have taken the money?

Turns out, not that many. According to Christa, "On average about 1.5 percent [take the $2,000]. It's really low. One of the side benefits about it is that people are actually more committed [to their jobs]."

What Christa Foley and Zappos are doing is certainly uncommon business practice, but it is one of the things that makes working at Zappos a truly unique experience. And the benefits don't stop at the end of the day. The company leaders aren't interested in employees who want to simply punch a time card—they want employees to feel like they belong to a community, which is why they have developed a program called Culture Fit. The Culture Fit philosophy is the backbone of the social experience at Zappos and is the reason that everyone in the office is more than just an employee.

As Christa says:

> When we are doing the culture evaluation, we are looking at our ten core values. One of these is to build a positive team and family spirit. During interviews, we ask if someone socializes with coworkers outside of the office, because we're really not looking for someone who is going to come in, do their job, and go home. For one, they won't really be connected to the organization and two, we have a philosophy—a belief—that if you're really passionate about something, it's not going to feel like work. So, you won't feel this division between personal and work.
>
> Most of the creative things we've done at Zappos didn't come from when we were in the office between 8:00 A.M. and 5:00 P.M., they've come from after-hours events, like drinks or while traveling to see a fashion show. We want people who are really open to that philosophy. Yes, we do lose out on some talented employees for whom this culture isn't a good fit, but we stick by our core values

and don't bring anyone onboard who isn't going to be a match. In the short term, talented people will be great, but in the long term they are going to be a pain in the ass if they don't fit with our culture.

When it comes to socializing with coworkers, I recommend having an open mind about everyone around you. You never know when someone who is really quiet may actually be incredibly fascinating. You have to give everyone a chance and not jump to conclusions or trust your assumptions. Don't put up a wall because you don't want to be someone's BFF on day one. You don't have to be. But you do have to make an effort. And that effort, and ability to step outside of your own comfort zone, could lead to some surprising career developments.

Modern Manners Guy's Top 10 Tips for Socializing at Work

Tip #1: Dining with Coworkers

Dining with coworkers is a great way to build camaraderie and it's usually the only time of the day when you can unwind and take off your "corporate jacket" for an hour. In one of my previous jobs, I'd meet up with a group of coworkers to grab a coffee or lunch in the company cafeteria every day. It was always the best part of the day. Dining with coworkers lets you learn a lot about people that you never knew (and maybe never even considered).

For example, perhaps you'd be surprised to find out that quiet Jeannie from accounting has a black belt in karate, or that snobby Tom volunteers at a dog shelter on the weekends. Spending time with colleagues outside the workplace is a valuable opportunity because it allows for closer interaction and helps you develop a better and more confident professional personality. However, sometimes these dining episodes can quickly go south, and fast.

When dining with coworkers, you can (and should) let your hair down a bit; however, remember that you're still "at work," even if you're in the neighborhood pizza joint. Should we really bet Mike $5 that he can't catch a meatball in his mouth after tossing it up in the air? I want to say "Yes" so badly because we all know that it will splatter across his face, which is hilarious, but the proper—and professional—answer is of course "No."

The bottom line is that even if you're dining with some of your best work friends, you're still in a professional environment. You're amongst coworkers, even managers, and so should behave more formally than you would at your annual Super Bowl party. Here are five go-to tips to remember:

1. Wait for everyone to arrive before ordering. The only caveat to this rule is if someone is going to be substantially late. In this case, you can always start with appetizers until they arrive. If they are going to be more than thirty minutes late, you can proceed with the meal.

2. Don't order a messy meal that makes you look like a contestant at the annual Nathan's Hot Dog Eating Contest. Stick to a manageable sandwich, salad, or an entrée that can be easily eaten with a fork and knife. Avoid the Sloppy Joe.

3. Wait until everyone gets their meal before you start eating. And when your plate arrives, don't dive at it like a rabid dog on a bone.

4. Allow your colleagues (especially the ladies) to order first.

5. Place a napkin in your lap.

The general precepts of personal hygiene and etiquette should remain intact when eating with colleagues. You not only want to keep your area of the table—and yourself—neat, but also your conversation. This isn't the time or the place to announce what you would like to "do" to the smokin' hot waiter or waitress that is serving you.

Tip #2: Splitting the Bill

Allow me to paint you a picture of a very typical situation: You and three coworkers go to lunch. You have a soup and soda totaling $5. Your colleagues have an entrée and a drink totaling $15 each. At the end of the meal, someone—who will inevitably be a repeat offender—blithely says, "Alright, that's $50 plus tip . . . So everyone just put in $20 and we're good to go." Whoa, what was that? That, my friends, is the sound of you getting screwed.

It's unfair and downright impolite to have others subsidize your meal. Unless it's a special occasion and I'm treating you or hosting the dinner, I don't want to be responsible for your gluttony. There are two major things that bother me about people who always want to split the bill:

1. They take advantage of you by using the excuse of "let's just split it" so they can save a few bucks. What, you think they didn't see their much larger meal next to yours? They did. And they're being a complete ass about it by trying to dupe you into paying for them.

2. People suck at simple math. Ever watch someone look at a receipt like it's Egyptian hieroglyphics, trying to decipher it? Everyone has a smartphone these days with a calculator on it that can easily count what each person at the table owes. Don't let someone skip out on paying their fair share just because they say, "Ah, screw it, I can't figure this out. Let's just split it." Most of the time, this is the moron from Example #1.

   Not only is this tasteless, it is also foolish because it assumes that everyone is on the same financial footing. Someone may have ordered a smaller meal because they weren't that hungry or because they simply couldn't afford it. I recently went to a dinner meeting at a high-end restaurant with two extremely wealthy people. I could not afford to eat the way they could: pricey appetizer, $60 steak, two glasses of wine, and an extravagant dessert. So I kept to a reasonable limit that would not make me seem rude, nor force me to call my credit card company for a balance increase. Thankfully they didn't notice or care. But they also didn't jump to "Let's split it" when the bill arrived.

When someone clearly orders less than others in your group, only to end up spending much more than they ever planned because some joker said, "Let's split it," it's a clear violation of everything mannerly. Plus it's just tacky.

The key to harmonious meals with coworkers is to just keep track of what you ordered, so you won't be surprised when the bill comes. If you know you've only spent $25 but the bill-splitter is telling you that you owe $75, play dumb. Ask, "Geez, how can that be when my entrée was $20 and I didn't have any drinks or appetizers? Are you sure the bill is right?" At that point Joe Order the Whole Menu will be shamed into rethinking his bill-splitting strategy.

"Okay, so there are four of us here. Split evenly, that's $125 a person. You guys want to do cash or credit?"

If the discrepancy between what you ordered and what you owe is a small amount—say, a few dollars—then you should just let it go. In the end, having to divide up that little amount will just be a hassle for everyone and make you look petty. However, when splitting the bill puts you seriously into the red, you have to say something. I find that the people who try to pull this crap do so repeatedly and you don't want to get caught in their pattern. So look at the bill, do your own math, and then decide if it's worth saying something. If it is, don't make a federal case. Keep it light, make a joke, and simply put down the amount for which you are responsible. This way, you are making a firm stand that this will not happen again.

Tip #3: Cliques

When we think of cliques, we tend to imagine the cool kids in high school—the jocks, the pretty people, the mean girls, the rebels, etc. Basically, everything that makes teen movies so epic. But workplace cliques are not at all like what you experienced in high school, they are much more professional and mature . . . or not.

It's only natural to be drawn to certain people who have a lot more in common with you. Maybe they work on the same projects, or enjoy talking about the same things, or are closer to your age. Regardless of the reason, you will ultimately prefer to be around some colleagues more than others, just like in your personal life.

Some say that office cliques are bad for the workplace because they foster isolation or alienation; however, that's only the case if people act like they're twelve. Cliques are in fact healthy for the office setting. After all, if you have a stressful day or screw up an assignment, isn't it always easier to commiserate with someone who understands what you're going through? That's what your office clique does.

The one caveat is if the clique turns into a closed circle where no new members are welcome. This *is* something that will breed isolation and alienation and should not be allowed at all. When you do form your core group of friends at work, don't maintain a members-only policy. If you happen to be heading out to lunch and pass a fellow coworker in the hallway, invite them along. If you are going out for someone's birthday, ask if anyone else would like to join. This way you won't get a bad reputation that will likely follow you all the way to HR.

> People are motivated when their leader knows them well and is approachable. On the other hand, it's problematic to be too close to those who work for you because the emotional drama can be terrible. Employees can also take their position for granted because they can feel like they don't have to perform if they are buds with the boss. So the goal is to be right in the middle. I try to always have personal relationships with those who work for me while keeping a safe enough distance where they know that business comes first.
>
> —Sam Tarantino, cofounder and CEO of Grooveshark

Tip #4: Casual Talk

I have a confession to make: I curse . . . a lot. I'm not proud of it and I'm trying very hard to fix it. However, I believe that sometimes dropping a colorful four-letter word is the only thing that'll get the point across. There is one stipulation to this belief: It's all about timing and location. For starters, cursing at the TV umpire for yet another bad call during the World Series is OK; cursing loudly in public or around kids is just tacky. And of course, you have to be extra careful with your language in a professional setting.

Don't get me wrong, there will be plenty of occasions when coworkers will annoy you, tempers will flare, you'll get into a heated debate, and want to rant like the filthiest sailor in the seven seas. But . . . you can't. Your boss might let a few choice words fly, but as the junior person in the group, you simply don't have that luxury.

Say you're in a meeting with your colleagues and Bill veers from reviewing the latest marketing analysis to a recap of a *Mad Men* episode. You'll probably want to lean to the person next to you and whisper, "What the f—k is Bill talking about?" Just be judicious. If the coworker is a friend and you know they're comfortable with your language, that's fine. But what if the colleague is someone you don't know quite as well? What if they take offense and complain to their boss about your inappropriate language? Why take the chance? Whatever you do, just keep it quiet because cursing out loud is absolutely unacceptable in a meeting scenario. When you curse, it shows a lack of control and professionalism. Neither of which is good for your bottom line.

Additionally, not everyone may get your sense of humor. The best comedians are able to utilize swear words in a way that fits the punch line beautifully. It's like how an artist adds the right touch of a certain color to accent a shadow in a painting. Is it essential? Maybe not. But when it's there, it just makes sense and you couldn't imagine the piece without it.

Guaranteed, at your office there will be at least one person who curses way too much and thinks they are hilarious:

"So the other day, this f——n guy was in front of me, ordering a f——n turkey sandwich and he starts ordering it with all kinds of f——n toppings and s—t. I was like, hold the f—k up, my man!"

This isn't funny, isn't cool, and simply shows you have no class and a tiny . . . vocabulary. When we curse, we tend to do so to prove a point or emphasize one. So if you use it all the time, it loses its meaning, its power, and its emphasis. Choose your words wisely to make sure they have the maximum impact. In the end, cursing in the office is usually a turnoff. It doesn't always land the way it was meant to and some words can be downright offensive. If you have to curse, only do it in private, with someone you trust who doesn't mind, or when you are by yourself and away from others.

The only exception is if you spill hot coffee on yourself . . . because when that happens, you can't help but let rip a few choice expletives. In that case, everyone will understand.

The Pros Weigh In: SPIKE MENDELSOHN
Owner of Good Stuff Eatery and We, The Pizza, former cast member of Bravo's *Top Chef*

• • •

When it comes to socializing with coworkers, there is no better experience than dining. It doesn't matter if it's in the small kitchen of your office, at a nearby coffee shop, or at a five-star restaurant (if the latter . . . are you hiring?).

And if you're reading this and saying you're too busy for lunch . . . you're not. No one is that important that they can't take a little time out for a meal.

Make time.

It's called being social.

If you still want to put up the facade of "all-work-no-play" then make it a working lunch. There, happy?

If there is one type of person who knows how to make people feel comfortable in social settings, it's a chef. After all, a chef makes a living by pleasing people's tastes and sensing what works for them and what doesn't. That's why I scored an interview with one of the coolest cats to don the double-breasted white chef's coat, Spike Mendelsohn. You may know Spike as the fast-talking, eclectic cast member of Bravo's *Top Chef,* or if you're lucky enough to visit one of his famous restaurants Good Stuff Eatery and We, The Pizza. Spike has been in the culinary industry his entire life, from working with his family to running posh kitchens in Europe. Now, his restaurants in the heart of our nation's capital have become hotbeds for office dwellers coming in droves to taste the delicious items from his menu. So Spike is used to observing colleagues socializing over a good meal.

> *I recommend that you find someone who you can look up to as a mentor. So many young people venture into the working world thinking that their ideas are new, innovative, and therefore bet-*

ter. But, let me tell you, we can all learn a thing or two from those who have been in the business for a while. I am lucky enough that my mom has been a mentor to me. She knows more than I ever will. Even if I disagree, or know that she is wrong, hearing the old-school approach or having a second perspective always has its benefits.

Any chance you have to grab someone who has something to teach you for a meal or just a cup of coffee, you should take full advantage of it and use the time as an opportunity to build your professional confidence.

Everyone has different tastes. If you don't know the associate too well, pick a restaurant with a menu that satisfies all palates. The restaurant doesn't need to be fancy or the new it-spot, but quality food and a nice ambiance go a long way.

Note from Modern Manners Guy: For the record, having dined at Spike's restaurants, I can tell you there is nothing better than Spike's Toasted Marshmallow Milkshake. Yes, his burgers and pizza can only be described as heaven on a plate, but the fat kid in me loves a good milkshake. So after downing two (one at my meal and one in the car ride home) I can tell you I left Good Stuff Eatery feeling amazing and ashamed at the same time, which is the ultimate sign of a good meal.

Tip #5: The Office Locker Room

For as long as I can remember, going to the gym has been a constant in my life. Whether it's free weights or cardio, finishing a workout is incredibly satisfying and rewarding. When I started at my current job, I discovered an amazing gym on the first floor open to all employees. Working out with coworkers is a great way to bond, knock out some stress, and talk about work in a much more casual setting. However, nothing can ruin a good workout like seeing your colleagues breaking every gym etiquette rule as if there was a contest to see who could be the most foul.

Yes, the locker room is meant for showering and changing, but the office gym is not your personal bathroom. I mean, towels were invented for a reason—use one! Don't walk around like the star of a National Geographic documentary. Even if you have, um, gifts that would make most doctors gasp and say, "Nurse, get my sketchpad! I have to document this," the gym is not the place to shake what your momma gave you.

Unless the building is on fire, or you are on fire and you don't have time to put a towel on, I suggest wrapping one around you before starting up a friendly convo with your colleagues. Same goes for when you are doing your hair at the sink. Just put your pants on—I beg you! Your hair won't get messed up if you take three seconds to zip up. And should you be on the receiving end of a colleague (or even your boss) who decides it's a good idea to strut their stuff in the communal locker room, simply hand them a towel and say casually, "Hey, here you go. I grabbed two by accident."

Now, ladies and gentlemen, if you are among those people who find washing your hands too much of a chore, please stay away from the office locker room. My four-year-old daughter knows to wash her hands after using the restroom, but apparently this rule has been forgotten by some adults. I was in the company locker room after a workout once and I saw a colleague come in to use the bathroom. He wore his weight-lifting gloves into the stall, did his business, and walked right back out to the gym. You can bet that those gloves have soaked up enough germs to make our friends at the CDC want to confine them to an isolated glass room in their laboratory.

Remember what I said about making first and lasting impressions on the people at your office? (See chapter 1.) Well, this goes double for when you are at the office gym. If you don't wash your hands, you can bet someone will notice and word will spread . . . just like those germs (sorry, I had to go there). The office locker room does not offer the same freedom as your gym locker room. Your colleagues don't want to see you naked. Well, maybe that one person in accounting who keeps sending you e-mail invitations to see their awesome antique marbles collection, but otherwise, no one.

Tip #6: Gift-Giving

During the holidays, many companies like to have an interoffice gift exchange amongst the staff. It's a great way to socialize, build morale, and ring in some holiday cheer after a long, hard year. These gift exchanges usually go one of two ways: very well or extremely badly. (What, were you expecting something more profound?)

It seems that for whatever reason the biggest faux pas around gift exchanges occur when someone doesn't follow the rules of the game. For example, there is a classic episode of *The Office* where Michael Scott (played by Steve Carell) gets someone an iPod as a Secret Santa gift, even though the limit for gifts was set at $20. Then, when he receives an oven mitt from his Secret Santa, he flips out.

Here is a perfect example of how not following directions can make you look like a fool. Ironically, in just about every workplace, there is one person like Steve Carell's character who decides to derail the office holiday gift train to make themselves feel good about their own generosity. This never works.

Let's say the rules dictate that all Secret Santa participants must make cupcakes as their gift and instead, you bring a five-tier wedding cake. This will look like you are blatantly trying to outshine everyone else, and no one will appreciate that. Plus, you will make the person who receives your overblown gift feel incredibly guilty for playing by the rules and not returning the favor.

When participating in a holiday gift exchange, stick to the set guidelines. And if you still have the desire to give someone a gift in *addition* to the office-sanctioned one (maybe you are actually good friends outside of the office), then by all means, go for it. However, do that off hours and away from the workplace. You don't want to draw any additional attention and get tongues wagging.

But what if you are the new person on the team and haven't had a chance to get to know anyone yet? Suddenly, you're launched into the midst of the gift exchange. You pull a name out of a hat and it says "Carl." You find yourself wondering "Is that the guy in billing or the office manager?" How do you figure out what to get this almost-stranger? Well, you can stalk "Carl" or have his home bugged for info, but the best way is to actually talk to Carl. Shocking, right? Not really. Use the holidays as an opportunity to actually chat and build a better relationship, so you not only become better coworkers (or even friends), but also research what he'd like. Believe me, your coworker will be flattered when they open a gift from their Secret Santa and find that you bought them something that is linked to a conversation you had in the past. That shows you were listening and paying attention. Kudos!

Tip #7: Coworkers Selling Crap for Their Kids' School

Anyone who works in an office has inevitably had a coworker approach them about a raffle or sale that their child, niece, nephew, or neighbor is doing for school. From cookies, to pies, to wrapping paper, to popcorn, kids are asked to hustle all kinds of things to raise money for their chronically underfunded schools (and, of course, to win prizes).

I'm all for this. There is nothing wrong with a little entrepreneurial spirit at a young age. Plus, I'm the biggest sucker in the world for those cookies. However, the selling of these goods falls mainly on the parents, aunts, uncles, or even the older siblings, not on the kids. And this pressure turns perfectly amiable coworkers into aggressive, crazed salespeople who act as if winning this contest will fund their child's free ride to Harvard.

But before you double down for some chocolate chip cookies, make sure you know the ground rules for selling tickets to your little sister's school raffle. Never assume it's proper to set up your lemonade stand outside your cubicle and act like a carnival barker to hustle treats. The first step is to ask the boss if this is a sanctioned activity in the workplace. Make sure to let him or her know how much time you plan to dedicate to peddling your wares. After all, your work is more important than selling enough popcorn to win your niece a Hello Kitty purse.

Also, don't badger your coworkers. If you tell me once that you are selling something, I don't need to be reminded every ten minutes. If I say I'm not interested, stalking my office won't help the cause. It's rude to assume that everyone wants to shell out $20 for that five-pound tub of cookie batter. Ask once and that's all. If they are interested, they will come to you, I promise.

Tip #8: There's Something on Your Face

Artists say that inspiration can come from anywhere. And this topic was inspired by an experience I had of walking into a café with a blood-dotted tissue on my chin still hanging there from when I cut myself shaving that morning. I knew it was there while getting dressed, but forgot to remove it before leaving the house. It wasn't a huge gash or anything but I did clearly cut myself. And apparently the two college kids behind the register at the coffeehouse didn't seem to think it was a big deal . . . nor did the security guard at my work . . . nor did the four co-workers I ran into on the way in. Finally, a true friend said, "Dude, you've got a bloody tissue on your face." Where was he two hours ago?!

I understand it's tough to tell someone they have a foreign object stuck to their face, be it tissue or even a rogue booger. But let's be honest, much of the time you *know* the person didn't intend to walk around with something sticking to their nose. In fact, you can even hear their scream of shame (like my officemates did) once they are informed of the facial intruder.

Yes, it's wrong to rudely point and laugh at someone, but at the same time, when done properly, it can be a kindness that can truly save the person from further embarrassment. And we can all appreciate that! I understand that it may appear impolite to point out a booger in someone's nose, but we can all agree that letting them know is a lot better than allowing them to walk into a client meeting with an unsightly thing hanging from their chin.

So how do you tell someone they have a facial intruder? You have a few options. For starters, kindly whisper the person's name to get their attention or tap their arm when no one else is looking. Then look around and gently brush your hand across your nose, along with giving them the nod to indicate they have something in theirs. It's the international sign for "Dude, you've got a booger." Or, when no one is looking, get the person's attention and whisper, "Really quick, you have something in your nose." And just as fast, they will take care of it and it'll be done.

If these don't work, revert back to high school and pass a note. One time a colleague of mine had something in her nose during a meeting. To save her the embarrassment, I typed "Got something in your nose" on my phone and showed it to her under the table, as if I was sharing an important e-mail. Worked like a charm and she quickly took care of things without anyone noticing. In the end, people will be incredibly thankful to you for taking the time and having the courage to discreetly assist them (emphasis on *discreetly*).

Tip #9: Discussing Politics at Work

In any big election year in the United States, there's a time period from the spring to the fall when you can't go five minutes without being caught up in the hoopla of politics. And as it gets closer to the presidential election, the annoyance of politicians promising world piece, low gas prices, and affordable health care gets even worse. When you turn on the TV, it seems that every other commercial is about a political candidate vying for your vote and explaining why their opponent is Satan. And when you click over to Facebook, chances are the discussion on your wall reads like a drunken ramble of diverging views about various candidates.

Even just driving to work, there are signs upon signs posted everywhere about who is the right person for the job. And then, once you get to your workplace, the debates continue to heat up. Everyone has an opinion, and wouldn't you know it, *everyone* is correct!

I'm no political genius, but I know what I believe in and that's about where my desire to discuss politics ends. I know that others will disagree with me, but that's the beauty of living in America: we have the freedom to believe whatever we want and speak our minds. However, sometimes in the workplace, this liberty gets way, way, waaaaay out of hand and turns average employees into rude monsters.

For example, have you ever had a discussion with someone when all of a sudden they turn into the Incredible Hulk and start shouting at you? Or from the get-go, they feel their argument could only be made clear by ranting and raving like a madman? And when it comes to politics, people seem to get heated particularly quickly, which always turns into a match-up of who can be the loudest. I just don't get this tactic.

The minute you lose control, you lose all credibility. When you start yelling like a trader on the floor of the New York Stock Exchange in the 1990s, no one in the office will want to talk to you about politics, or anything else. It's highly unmannerly to argue with your coworkers in general, but getting into a shouting match in front of a roomful of colleagues is downright embarrassing!

Similar to a bar fight, if you really feel the need to duke it out, just take it outside, not into the office kitchen! If coworkers feel that they *have to* talk politics, then they need to do it only in designated areas—basically anywhere but at someone's desk, office, or the kitchen—as well as set times. When is this time? Well, that's for the big boss to figure out. I can only tell you when it's *not* a good time: in a meeting, on a conference call with clients, at a holiday party, at a group outing, or at a baby shower.

Lastly, the best way to avoid having a political uproar in the office is to simply not allow the conversations to start in the first place. At my friend's office, his boss was so superstitious about his favorite sports team winning the Super Bowl that every time someone even brought it up, they had to put $1 into a fishbowl as punishment. The money collected would go toward a pizza party during the game. This was not a ruse to get the employees to pay for pizza—it was a clever way to avoid a topic the boss had declared off limits during work hours. A brilliant idea!

Politics is not like the elephant in the room (no pun intended)—it is not something that *has to* be discussed. It has nothing to do with your job (unless you work at a campaign office) and therefore can be avoided during work hours. Or would you prefer to voice your opinion only to find that your boss disagrees completely and now thinks you are an idiot? Not worth it.

Tip #10: Office Snacking

Regardless of where you work it can be rough getting through a full day without completely feeling wiped out. So what do we do? We snack. I take my snacking very seriously. My colleagues know that when they come to my office, they'll encounter a buffet of pretzels, candy, peanuts, and other assorted treats.

Many companies have designated snacking areas that help keep smells and sounds to a central location. Sometimes it's in the kitchen, or in an empty cube no one is using, or even just a small bowl on the boss' desk. Snack areas are the workplace version of tailgating. People bring in treats and next thing you know, it's an all-out party. "What about that ten A.M. conference call? Nah, who cares, JoAnn brought in homemade cupcakes!"

But with snacks come wrappers, plates, napkins, utensils, etc., which all equal a lot of trash. Have you ever seen an office snack area after a big event? It looks like armageddon, with smeared remnants of JoAnn's cupcakes and Steve's apple turnover left in shambles as if savages just stormed through.

Apparently people forget their manners when it comes

time to chow down. Some set up camp at that rogue desk housing the tasty snacks, leaving wrappers on the floor for the cleaning people to find. After all, that's *their* job, right? No, it's not. It's a cleaning person's job to clean up, but not scrape frosting off the walls because you couldn't be bothered. Plus, it always shocks me when trash is left on tables or floors when there is a trashcan right in the area. Really, people?

When it comes to office snack etiquette, we must remember that we are adults, not toddlers at a birthday party. And the office is a place of business, not the Golden Corral on "All You Can Eat Tuesdays." Yes, your fellow coworkers were nice enough to bring in tasty treats, but you must still maintain a certain level of professionalism.

After all, you wouldn't show up to a meeting with a giant Doritos stain across your shirt, right? So why would you sabotage your space by leaving a mess? When you are snacking, be respectful of the office property and those around you. Use the trashcan. Wipe up whatever you spill and please, by all means, do not leave food out to rot and grow mold. Disgusting!

Additionally, office snacking is a communal activity. So if you do bring in snacks, it's always proper to share. If you have a large stack of printer paper you've been saving for when you run out, and your coworker needs some, you should share, right? If you have the only working stapler that doesn't get jammed, you should let others borrow it. And if you are taking part in office snacking, you should do your best to give back. I'm not saying you need to bring in a box of rare truffles from the South of France, but you should contribute something to the pot.

But before you head out to buy your snacks, make sure you consider the people around you. You don't want to be the person who brings in fancy organic energy bars made of potent rare spices only to start a chain reaction down the hall of, "What the f——k is that smell?" Stick with safe, dry options like pretzels, crackers, candy, etc. Avoid questionable snacks (don't roll your eyes at me, fried pork rinds *are* questionable).

"Listen, Walt, some of the other staff finds your snacking habits a bit . . . well, nauseating. Any chance you can switch to popcorn or pretzels?"

MODERN MANNERS GUY QUIZ

You are out to lunch with three of your coworkers. You colleagues order meals that cost $30 each, and your meal is only $10. When the check comes, someone says, "Let's just split it." This leaves you paying much more for what you ate. What do you do?

A Go with the flow and just cough up the extra dollars without saying anything. Stew in your own resentment.

B Do a "Dine and Dash" and find an excuse to bail before the bill comes.

C Put in $10, then as you go to reach for that extra $20, you pretend to faint and lie on the restaurant floor unconscious, hoping the distraction will get you out of paying more than you owe.

D Casually say, "Hey, guys, I only had that appetizer, so I'm going to put in $15. Sound good?"

Answer

D Always speak up when it comes to paying for what you owe. If the difference is just a couple of bucks (and you can afford it), then option A to go with the flow is fine. However, there comes a time when you are clearly being taken advantage of and that's not acceptable. You are not being a bad sport by paying only what you owe—you are being a responsible adult.

(What's that sound? Oh yeah, it's the sound of the crushing debt you've racked up while in college.)

It may feel uncomfortable to speak up, but when you are clearly getting ripped off it's worth standing up for yourself. The key is to say something casually without making a big issue out of it. Plus, if the people you are with can't do the level of math it takes to divide up the check fairly, you probably don't want to work with them.

MODERN MANNERS GUY SOCIALIZING AT WORK TOOL KIT

1 **ALWAYS PACK CHANGE.** When you dine out for lunch or dinner, most of the time a credit card is easiest and will be evenly used to split a bill. However, sometimes cash is king. I recommend having change for at least a $20 so if the bill comes, you can pay your exact amount and let the others worry about doing the math.

2 **PROPER SNACKS.** It's one thing to walk into a meeting chewing gum (just kidding . . . it's not cool at all), it's quite another to bring a full-blown snack tray. You won't starve if you don't eat for an hour. If you bring food into the office, keep it in sealed packages so others won't have to smell it. It's hygienic and neat and will save you some awkward stares, plus if you forget about something and it rots, at least the mold will be contained.

3 **THE SWEAR BET.** Just like in the classic *Simpsons* episode where they had a Swear Jar for Homer, I recommend instituting a tally point system amongst your colleagues so that the most severe curser of the week who racks up the most points has to buy donuts, pizza, or coffee for the entire crew on Friday afternoon. This way, you make light of the fact that people swear too much but also bring a positive resolution to the situation.

4 **MAP IT OUT.** One essential tool to have by your side is the gift of timing. Well, it's actually a skill, that when used properly is a gift for us all. When you are out to lunch or coffee with coworkers, put a reminder in your cell-phone calendar that beeps at a particular time alerting you that time is running out and you should head back soon. This way the group knows it's time to go, without having to watch the clock and you won't get a stern talking-to from the boss when you arrive back to work two hours late.

5 **DON'T SWEAT IT.** While in the gym with coworkers, you can't let your "true gym self" come out. So if you usually work out in skintight clothing, you should dress a bit more conservatively at the office gym. Cover up any tattoos or piercings that seemed like such a good idea when you were seventeen. If you are one of those gym grunters who tend to yell when you lift, put a lid on it at work. Save your maxing out on the bench for another time or when colleagues aren't around. For one, you look like a madman, with your face bulging red and the veins popping out. And two . . . well, there is no two. Just follow number one.

FIVE

Social Media at Work

Hey, watch who you're poking (and liking)!

Like it or not, we're being watched 24/7. There's a
smartphone trained on us constantly. A youthful indulgence
quickly goes viral. Social media and the wired world also
make us all ambassadors of our brand.

—Andrew Buerger, cofounder of B'more Organic

ach morning millions wake up to see what their
3,000 closest friends on Facebook have done since
last night. Did someone get a new job? Get engaged?
"Like" that photo you posted the other day? We can't
help ourselves. Facebook, Twitter, YouTube, Instagram,
Pinterest, LinkedIn, Google+ have all become a huge part
of our everyday life. You can't avoid it, and in fact, a day
without social media seems . . . odd, disjointed and, dare
I say it, lost. It's like cake without icing, sporting events
without drunken fans, or a bar mitzvah without "Gangnam
Style." And with all the attention we put on social media,

we have a hard time separating our real world from our digital world.

Navigating social media is a gradual learning process and so is how you use social media in the office. These days, potential employers often check out your Facebook page before extending that offer for the job or promotion. Even if you nailed the interview and had them practically cracking open the bottle of Champagne before you left, one quick look on your Facebook page could have all of that crumbling down.

Why? Oh, that's right, your old college friend just posted those championship party pictures where you're hanging from the top of a goal post—wearing only your underwear and a smile—as a squad of police officers wait for you at the bottom. Now, if that doesn't scream "Employee of the Month" I don't know what does.

Every workplace has its own interpretation of what is acceptable use of social media. Some embrace it and allow employees to do whatever they like at all times, while others block the sites behind a firewall and totally ban access to social media during work hours. Even if you work *on* social media as your job, the way you conduct yourself now that you are in a professional setting is drastically different from how you could prior to setting foot inside the office. Unfortunately, a lot of what you consider "fun" has to be reevaluated as you move forward in your professional career. Whereas your main priority in your social life was making sure all those "friends" knew your every thought and action throughout the day, in the business world if you want to be treated like a professional, you have to manage your social network wisely.

Don't get me wrong—you can still post that hilarious party photo or the smart-ass comment about your friend that you can't resist, but you do have to step back and consider the consequences. That picture of you streaking across the parking lot last New Year's Eve while holding a bottle of tequila? Maybe not the best display of professionalism. Same thing goes for how you represent yourself on Twitter and LinkedIn. I say this because once you enter a corporate environment, you are a direct representative of the company and they won't tolerate someone

"Dude, I just tweeted this hashtag #getanewjob!"

who posts hate-filled rants, even if you claim that you're just being funny and sarcastic. They won't ask for an explanation.

Luckily, there are ways to use social media for work and for fun without losing your job and your sense of humor.

The Pros Weigh In: NEIL BLUMENTHAL
Cofounder of Warby Parker

• • •

I love it when a company brings ingenious innovation to a product that seems very common, like eyeglasses, for example. Most people think that the secret to success is to just make a sweet pair of shades and hope celebrities start wearing them. And they're right much of the time. But my friends at Warby Parker have taken an entirely different approach that has totally reinvented the industry. Instead of chasing celebrities, they encourage real people who buy and wear their glasses to become part of the Warby Parker team. One way they did this was by kicking off a cross-country road trip with an old-school school bus whose interior was stacked with oak shelves, a chalkboard, a library of books, and a full selection of Warby Parker frames, manned by its own staff. Known as the Warby Parker Class Trip, the goal of the event was to bring the Warby Parker experience directly to their customers all across the country. The team wanted to make sure everyone knew they were coming to town, so they launched an epic social media campaign on Facebook, Twitter, and Instagram. It was a huge hit.

Since the folks at Warby Parker have mastered the art of social media, I wanted to chat with one of the founders, Neil Blumenthal, and hear his thoughts on the etiquette of social media in the office.

Neil told me that even though employees are encouraged to interact on the Web with fans and other companies, there is a fine line between what is appropriate and what isn't off limits. The Warby Parker team takes their reputation seriously and knows that one wrong post on social media could have a domino effect that negatively affects their brand.

> *We've been working on an internal social media policy. It's tough. Certainly employees can't speak about the company to the press without permission, but speaking in the public domain is encouraged. We want staffers to talk about their experiences and what they're learning and if they're having fun. It motivates them and increases productivity. It also helps us recruit more talent and acquire more customers. But there is a fine line between what is appropriate to share publicly and what is off limits. We want our people to exercise their better judgment.*

Along with making sure employees clearly understand that "fine line"—which is different for every company—the management of Warby Parker puts a lot of emphasis on every potential employee's social media presence before they commit to bring them onto the team.

> *We are selective about choosing the people who work for us. We want to see if the person has good judgment or not because the lines are so blurred and ill-defined between what is a private conversation and what is in the public domain when it comes to social media. [When we're considering a candidate] how they represent themselves on social media carries as much weight as their references.*

Modern Manners Guy's Top 10 Tips for Using Social Media at Work

Tip #1: Facebook Etiquette, Part 1—In the Public Eye

Coworkers may not be the closest people in your life, but on an average day, you'll see your coworkers more than anyone else—including your spouse, siblings, parents, or children. So it's natural for us to want to "friend" our coworkers on social media. However, some people forget that when you invite people into your Facebook world, you are letting them see a very personal side of your life.

Let's make one thing perfectly clear: Facebook is public. If you post your e-mail address, expect to be e-mailed. If you post a photo of yourself, don't be upset if someone comes across it and makes their opinion known. Think of Facebook as a giant conference with everyone you know in attendance—and every time you post something, it's as if you just hopped up on stage and loudly announced it to the entire room.

One thing that people tend to forget is that Facebook is date- and time-stamped (to the minute). Why does this matter? Well, say you're in a meeting, supposedly listening to an important presentation, but instead you're posting a status update about your team's overtime win on your Facebook wall. While your eyes are saying "I hear you. Good point!" your Facebook timeline is saying, "I really don't care what is going on in this meeting right now." If you work for a company that routinely checks employees' social media profiles (and many do), you better believe someone will notice and it won't be long before the Powers That Be find out. How are you going to explain that?

> Your personal life and your work life should not be a Venn diagram. Of course you can put pictures on your desk and have small talk with your coworkers, but leave it at that. If you have the burning desire to post something on Facebook, make it about your family or friends. And do it after work. I work from home and if I sign into Facebook in the middle of the day and see people logged in, my first thought is, "Somebody doesn't have a lot to do at work." I mean, that's why *I'm* on Facebook at 2:20 p.m.
>
> —Benjamin August, screenwriter, producer, and casting director

Tip #2: Facebook Etiquette, Part 2—To Friend or Not to Friend?

It can be hard to say no to friend requests—whether they come from someone you haven't seen since your third-grade class portrait, from a kooky relative you wouldn't even talk to at Thanksgiving, or your colleague. Never fear, there are ways to reject a friend request without looking like a jerk.

One easy way to deal with an unwanted friend request is to actually go ahead and accept the person but block them from seeing your updates or, even better, from you seeing theirs. That way they aren't gaining a lot of access to your profile and you've saved them the embarrassment of rejection. And if you choose not to see their updates, they'll be out of sight, out of mind. It'll be as though you never became virtual friends in the first place. Just realize that if you block them from seeing your posts, they'll probably notice eventually. Then you can just say that you don't have much time to post anything, what with all the *work* you have to do.

Another easy fix if you worry about your potentially embarrassing friends making you look bad to your colleagues is to create a separate Facebook account that you use for business only. That way you'll have a clean Facebook page for professional use and you'll still be able to keep tabs on your crazy friends via your personal page. This way you can accept a friend request from a colleague you don't necessarily like by connecting with them on your business-only Facebook account.

In the end, you don't owe anyone access to your Facebook page. Will they be mad at you if you don't accept their friend request? Maybe. But is avoiding a little tension worth sacrificing your professional reputation and livelihood? No, it's not. Plus, let's be honest, of all your Facebook friends, how many do you see regularly? I'm talking daily or weekly. Probably not that many. So if you don't want to be around someone in real life, does it make sense to invite them into your personal online world? Life will go on if that person does not get a friend acceptance from you. Chances are, if you're waffling on accepting them, they were not a real friend in the first place.

Tip #3: Twitter Etiquette

I love Twitter! My Modern Manners Guy followers on Twitter are fantastic! But not everyone is like me. I find that Twitter tends to be polarizing: either you love it or you hate it. There is hardly ever a middle ground. And those who fall into the "love" category are quick to point out when one of the "haters" don't follow proper Twitter etiquette (Twetiquette?).

I don't think we need to go into the details of tweets gone bad . . . but then again, it is kind of fun. From Congressman Anthony Weiner's embarrassing wiener photos (yeah, that was a good idea!), to random drunk tweets from every corner of the world, people keep forgetting that once something goes live on Twitter it goes *live*! Yes, you can delete a tweet, but if someone already saw it (as was the case with Anthony

Weiner and the savvy journalist who picked it up) it stays on their feed, until they refresh or scroll away. And, of course, you can take a screen shot of a tweet to use as ammo in perpetuity. In some cases it's a good idea to let those who tweeted improperly suffer the consequences (yes, you, Mr. Weiner). But in all cases, the best thing to do is to just watch what you send out into the Twittersphere.

Ranting online is easy. We all have giant keyboard muscles sitting behind that computer. We also assume that everyone will get our sense of humor, no matter how morbid or bizarre. But when it comes to Twitter, it's key to remember Thumper's rule: "If you can't say something nice, don't say nothing at all." So if you think you are going to offend someone, chances are they will be offended and you will look like a bully.

Before you click "Tweet," consider what you've just written through the eyes of your boss. If there's any chance he or she will read it and think you're a lunatic, it's probably not worth the 140 characters. And by the way, there is no law that says you have to tweet, nor is there a law that says you have to have followers. I have several Twitter accounts and one of these I use just to follow news trends. It's like reading the newspaper every day—you don't have to e-mail the writer and say you liked the article just because you read it. Twitter is an opt-in system. So if you are active, great! If not, no biggie. Just make sure that when you incorporate your Twitter world into your business world, you recognize that you're on a different playing field.

Tip #4: LinkedIn Etiquette

LinkedIn, unlike Facebook or Twitter, could very well be the reason why you got your job in the first place. It's the best way to search for job openings and find out who is who at the company of your choice. Perhaps the most important thing to remember about LinkedIn is that it's not the place to be goofy or wild—LinkedIn is meant for business. Period.

When presenting yourself on LinkedIn, you want to make sure you are doing so the same way you would present yourself in a professional setting. Do you accept everyone who wants to connect with you? The answer is yes—only *if* they meet your professional needs. That's the question you should continually ask yourself on LinkedIn. This doesn't mean only connecting with people in your field. You never know when a graphic design connection could help with business cards, or a lawyer connection could advise you on a legal question. With LinkedIn I tend to be more inclusive. Since you have far less daily interaction with people on LinkedIn—and those interactions tend to be mainly professional in nature—connecting with someone who may not be exactly in your industry doesn't pose much of a threat. That's why my default response to people who request to connect with me is "yes."

However, there are exceptions. You don't want to be linked with someone who has a sketchy background or a questionable reputation. That one bad connection can ruin a lot of the good ones. If you get invited to connect by someone who has "shady" written all over them, simply

reject their request. You do not have to provide an answer
for your decision. If the person is hitting you up for a contact or a meeting and uses a request to do so, you can still
answer their question in a message without accepting their
connection request. Is that weird? Maybe. Then again, it's
your reputation on the line, not theirs, so you make the call.

One other thing I should mention about LinkedIn:
Joining a group of like-minded professionals is a great way
to network. However, LinkedIn is not the place to overwhelm people with your views. The groups on LinkedIn
are there to share advice and news, not to fight and argue.
Leave that for a rogue page on Facebook.

Tip #5: Photo-sharing Etiquette

Without fail, almost weekly, I go on Facebook and see
posted on my news feed a message that says, "You have
got to see this!" So I click to open the image only to find
a photo someone posted of a friend or family member not
looking their best. This has happened to all of us and most
of the time, as soon as we see the picture, we immediately
wish the person had thought twice before posting.

I know what you're thinking: What could be the harm
of posting the drunken shot of Cousin Walter passed out
at a New Year's party, seconds away from urinating himself? However humorous you may find a photo, you have
to be prepared for what will happen after it goes live to
the world. What if Cousin Walter's boss sees that picture?
What if it is deemed inappropriate behavior by his stodgy

managers and Walter gets canned? How is he going to provide for his family and pay his kids' college tuition? Do you really want to live with this guilt hanging over your shoulders? I didn't think so.

Do you think the creators of Photoshop realized how powerful their tool would become for humiliating people? I doubt when they were coding they envisioned the end result would be some teenager turning his father into a zombie. Yes, Photoshop is used to enhance a photo—to make it nicer (or nastier)—but nowadays, people throw pretty much anything into Photoshop, add a funny quote, a piece of clip art, click "send all," and voila, it's an instant online hit!

For some reason, people's sense of humor tends to increase with some not-so-friendly editing. Remember that photo of your best friend at his holiday party doing karaoke to "It's Raining Men"? Well, now with Photoshop you can easily add in all the other Village People to complete the band. And I'm sure that's just what your buddy wanted floating around his workplace.

Trust me, no one in the office will appreciate your sense of humor if you make them appear heavier than they are, drunker than they were or, even worse, by pasting a racist, sexist, or otherwise offensive saying above their head. As I said before, once you post something online, it has a life of its own and if it goes viral it's hard to stop. So next time you consider posting an image online, realize that by trying to be funny, you might just close the door on a friendship—or worse, a job.

Tip #6: YouTube Etiquette

Tip #5 has an evil sibling and it's what I refer to as "That Awesome YouTube Video." Here's how it goes: I'm at work going through my e-mail first thing in the morning and I start to hear some chatter down the hall, when it quickly turns into full-blown laughter. Ten seconds later, I get an e-mail about a video that must be opened immediately. And thus, we have that awesome YouTube video that has made its way around the office like the flu. And like that nasty seasonal virus, you can't avoid the awesome YouTube video, you can only hope to minimize its effects.

Because we're social creatures, it's only natural to want to share something funny. Whether it's an old person falling off a chair, a cat spinning on a record player, or an awful wedding dance video, we can't help but want to press "send" and share the good times with others. Except here's the rub: What's funny to some, may not be funny to all.

Sending a video around the office—regardless of how funny you think it is—always ends up being a nightmare, because you never know who it will offend. And even if it's entirely inoffensive (a cat spinning on a record player, come on!), there will inevitably be people who will find it a distraction. When a video is blaring and people are laughing loudly, someone will likely complain because all your cackling has disrupted their phone call or client meeting.

One more thing: Never send a video to someone's work e-mail. Many friends of mine work in the government sector and their workplace networks are equipped with programs that scan e-mails for suspicious content. One colleague sent a video around for a pop song by Ke$ha called "Blow" and you could only imagine how fast that was flagged. Needless to say the word "blow" in a government e-mail attracts the watchdogs pretty quickly. She got a phone call from security thirty minutes later, and after she explained herself they gave her a verbal warning and treated her like a toddler in preschool who just got busted for eating crayons.

Your best bet for sharing that awesome YouTube video is to: 1) E-mail it off hours to and from personal e-mail addresses. 2) Don't cause a circle of madness at your desk with everyone hanging out, laughing their butts off. 3) Always, always assume there will be at least one buzz-kill in the office who will think the video of a father being hit in the crotch by his six-year-old isn't funny at all. (For the record, crotch-shot videos are *always* funny. Just not at work.)

The Pros Weigh In: SAM TARANTINO
Cofounder and CEO of Grooveshark
• • •

Grooveshark is an amazing online community that provides free music streaming, online radio stations, and connects with artists and friends. Over the years, Grooveshark has allowed millions of people to turn their favorite music into a social experience, connecting their playlists to sites like Facebook and Twitter. CEO Sam Tarantino is serious about the impact of social media in the workplace.

He understands the difficulties of balancing our social media worlds with our professional lives.

> *[When it comes to social media,] everyone here at Grooveshark is pretty respectful of one another. We are still a small company so we treat each other like family, and I'm very proud of that. If someone is being problematic we confront them directly about it before it gets out of hand.*

The concept of social media manners at work goes right to the top. The company leader sets the tone for what is appropriate and what is taboo. It's a constant balancing act and it's up to every employee (aka, you) to pay attention to the signals coming from upper management. If you aren't sure that something you're posting online is 100 percent kosher with your boss, don't risk losing your job. Either rephrase or just don't go there.

Tip #7: Tasteless Photo Tagging

Maybe it was a fun night out, a great holiday party, or a perfect beach day with the family—no matter the event, nothing holds sweet memories like a good photo. And nothing can completely ruin your day like seeing a photo of yourself in a rare fail.

We all have that one Facebook "friend" who arrived seemingly out of nowhere. His friend request appeared in your inbox one fine morning and you thought, "Well, time has passed; they've probably matured. Why not?" But the next thing you know, you're tagged in a photo from spring break fifteen years ago singing "Livin' on a Prayer" four margaritas deep at Señor Frog's. It was hilarious at the time but now, when you are trying to establish yourself as a responsible executive, reliving that moment—in public—is not quite so hilarious. The response to tasteless photo tagging? Kindly but firmly request that the offender untag the picture, and then unfriend them. If they refuse, report the photo to Facebook and they'll untag it for you.

No matter how funny it may seem, never tag—or post—an unflattering photo of someone else. You never know what kind of domino effect can follow. When in doubt, ask first.

Tip #8: Reply All . . . and Other Ways to Tank Your Career

While thinking about the title for this book, I made a list of all the instances in my career when I had to remove my foot from my mouth. It was a very long list. Luckily, I did learn from my mistakes. But whether I called the boss by the wrong name, walked in late to a meeting, forgot to show up at all, or decided that staying out until 3:00 A.M. when I had a meeting at 7:00 the next morning was a good idea, nothing, and I mean *nothing* was worse than replying all to an e-mail.

True story: My colleague Dave works in a conservative financial services firm. One day, he received an e-mail about a company summer picnic from the HR manager. In the e-mail, it explained that the picnic would have a Wild West theme and that everyone had to bring food in line with the theme (chili, pit beef, corn, etc.). Since the person who sent the e-mail was a friend and shared the same sense of humor, Dave felt comfortable replying: "Wild West? I'm going to bring in baked beans and have everyone reenact the campfire scene from *Blazing Saddles*! We'll be farting our brains out the entire meal! It will be epic!" He pressed "Send" and off it went . . . to the inbox of every single employee of the company. Turns out he hit "reply all" instead of just "reply."

The best part was that he didn't realize it right away. He heard people laughing from several cubes away but didn't think much of it. Then when he walked down the hallway, one coworker greeted him with "Yippee kay-ay, pardner!"

"Odd," he thought, "but whatever, that guy is odd." A few seconds later, another colleague popped out of his office to make farting noises with his hands pressed against his mouth.

"Totally immature," Dave figured, but again nothing struck a chord.

A few minutes later, Dave's smartphone beeped and he saw a text from his friend in HR that said, "Way to go . . . you hit reply ALL."

Just like that, all the air in his lungs completely evaporated. He ran out of the building to his car and just sat inside motionless wondering, "Did I just send 400 people, including the CEO, an e-mail about . . . farting?!?!" Yes, yes he did.

Let this be a warning. Always, always, always check the "To" line of an e-mail before you click "Send." Remember, there are two options: "reply" and "reply all." One will keep you safe and the other could ruin your career. It took about a month for people to forget about Dave's e-mail, not to mention the stern talking-to that he received from the CEO about appropriate company communication. The good news is that he's since rebounded from the experience and it's safe to say he'll never click "reply all" again.

Tip #9: Embarrassing E-mails and Texts

Let's say you weren't careful and you did in fact click "reply all" when responding to a mass e-mail. And let's say that your response included language that was less than professional. What do you do? Well, cursing at your phone or computer screen like Samuel L. Jackson in *Pulp Fiction* is step one. But once you're done with that, you realize that your message was still delivered. That's why step two is to accept that unless DeLorean starts mass producing actual time machines, you can't go back in time and unsend. All you can do is try to recover some integrity.

An embarrassing text or e-mail is usually the result of something incredibly frustrating. It's a quick-trigger reaction when you need to vent. But telling your coworker or boss where they can "go" or what to "stick" and "where" is beyond rude and of course a professional crash. These kinds of texts or e-mails always come back to haunt you—especially since come new-job-search time your potential new employer will most likely call your old employer to ask about your performance. *Awwwwwkward!*

So how do we minimize the damage? The only way to put this behind you is to be honest, accept blame, and grovel a bit. The boss will respect you more for your honesty than for trying to BS your way out of it. Keep it clear, simple, and don't dwell on the details. "I was wrong to send that message and I know it. It was a very poor decision and will never happen again. Hopefully you can accept my sincerest apology." That's it. Whatever you do, do not cast blame. "I was really tired and overworked," "My kid was up all night and I didn't get enough sleep," "She started it!" All of these are lame and petty. Just fall on the sword and be done with it.

One last thing: Unless your boss is fifteen, never text them something important—it's tacky. Instead, send a well-thought-out e-mail or just pick up the phone (it's that plastic thing with buttons gathering dust on your desk).

Tip #10: Interoffice Online Wars

Regardless of how happy-go-lucky your office is, and no matter how many friends you have at work, there will undoubtedly be people with whom you bump heads. If you're an adult, which I hope you remember you are, you'll take a walk outside and decompress after a dispute or even vent to a friend (in private) about how rude someone was to you. Both are completely appropriate ways of handling a dispute. However, some people can't just leave work at work and so they take their interoffice war to the Internet, posting their frustration on Twitter or Facebook.

As we discussed earlier, it's pretty easy to be bold and brave online. And if you're not careful, things can quickly escalate and land right into harassment territory. It's not only rude to take to the airwaves when you are feuding with a fellow coworker, it also makes the company as a whole look bad—which, I promise you, will not go over well with the boss.

I worked in an office once where the environment was so strained, you could cut the tension with a knife. In any given meeting, you could see the front lines clearly drawn. Half the group would sit on one end of the conference table, closer to the manager, and the other half was as far away against the wall as possible to separate themselves. This is bad for productivity and morale and no manager wants to wind up with warring factions on his hands. That's why bad-mouthing and degrading a fellow coworker is not acceptable. Even though your social media accounts are not owned by your employer, when you bring their business into your personal life, it immediately becomes an issue.

If you're the victim of an interoffice social media war,

do not fight back—online, that is. Let that person who tweeted about your bad choice of winter hat look publicly foolish while you remain professional and composed. But don't immediately wave the white flag and surrender either. You need to calmly and coolly confront the person (in person) and tackle the issue head-on. Too ballsy? Maybe. But as I said in chapter 4, bullies need to be confronted directly (and social media haranguing is a form of bullying).

You won't always get along with everyone at your job, but you will have to tolerate them and play nice. And remember: You don't have to share everything with 3,000 of your "closest" friends. Some things should remain private.

MODERN MANNERS GUY QUIZ

While on Facebook, you see that a fellow coworker has posted the following to their wall: "Looks like Michelle got the promotion. I guess it helps that she's dating the head of HR. Screw that! I guess that means I should start wearing shorter skirts. I hate this place!" What should you do?

A You should reply with, "Nope, new clothes won't help. You still look like a gremlin."

B "Like" the comment.

C Write a post on their wall defending Michelle's merits and hard work. Make it very clear that her knowledge and skills are why she got the job.

D The next day, confront your coworker in person and advise her to reconsider expressing her feelings so openly on Facebook (or other social media sites) since everyone can see what she wrote—including her boss and Michelle.

Answer

D I'm constantly shocked when people forget this simple fact: Guys, it's public! It's live! And I promise you the offended person will find out (and likely retaliate in some way). When it comes to posting negative or gossipy work-related comments on your Facebook wall or Twitter feed, no matter how funny or how true, the firestorm this may cause (and I use the word *fire*storm purposely) will likely not justify the two minutes of joy you received from venting. Not to mention the fact that it makes your company look like it's operated by a bunch of catty teenagers. If you go on Facebook and claim that your company "sucks" or "is run by idiots," you should stop what you're doing, pack your stuff, and don't bother coming back in tomorrow because the idiots won't tolerate it.

MODERN MANNERS GUY'S SOCIAL MEDIA AT WORK TOOL KIT:

1 YOUR WORK NAME VS. YOUR *REAL* NAME. For those who must post their every thought on social media, I suggest creating a secondary account just for your business reputation. However, you'll need to alter your personal account so it's a little harder to find. Your professional account should be under the name that appears on your business card. Your personal account, the one you've had since college, should be tweaked. Your friends won't mind and this way you can still rant about your bad dates without compromising your professional demeanor.

2 OFFICE SOCIAL MEDIA POLICY. Many offices don't have a set social media policy. It's usually, "Look guys, don't post stupid pictures or talk about your coworkers on Facebook." And the company expects that to be the rule of thumb—which is a good one—but it's not enough. There must be a more thorough set of guidelines and you should ask your employer about them. If there is one, learn it and follow it. If there isn't one, do some research on what other companies in your industry are doing. If you find one that seems reasonable and makes sense, bring the idea to your boss and present it as an independent project that you worked on after hours. I guarantee your boss will eat it up with a spoon.

3 LIST OF SOCIAL MEDIA COWORKERS. Similar to the office phone list, make sure you know who is who on social media. Although it's not the best idea to talk about work on social media, this doesn't mean you can't be online friends with co-workers. That's why you should create a solid, up-to-date list of people's names as they appear on their social media accounts so you know it's them you are friending or following. This way you aren't wondering why Scott Smith who sits next to you hasn't accepted your friend request . . . because you sent the request to a Scott Smith who lives in another country and has no idea who you are.

SIX

Work Events Etiquette

It's party time! Who's next on the keg stand? . . .
and other ways to bomb your reputation.

> If you are passionate about something—follow that.
> It will make you happier and a great employee.
> Please don't worry about money. You'll eventually make
> money doing it, if you stick with it. I've been passionate
> about health for years, and I finally figured out a way
> to make money in the health food industry at age
> forty-five. I wish I had done it earlier.
> —Andrew Buerger, cofounder of B'more Organic

Throughout your career, and even in your first few months on the job, you will be asked to participate in various workplace-sponsored events. Some will be fun, like Friday night happy hours, coworkers' weddings, or baby showers. Others, like office retreats or conferences, will make you feel like you're on a hidden camera TV show and people are testing your limitations. Regardless of whether you're glad to attend or require a beta blocker to get through it, office events are mandatory—you have to be a team player even when you don't want to be.

Think of any work-sponsored event as a learning experience. You'll be surprised what you can learn from participating in something so tedious or uncomfortable that you find yourself contemplating pulling the fire alarm just to get away. There's a lot that goes on in work-sponsored events that can directly affect the future of your career. And that's where the learning comes in. I've been to countless events that I absolutely hated, but at nearly each one I learned something that made me better. So just go and make the best of it. Brush off the negative and embrace the positive. Plus, even the worst conference or office retreat will have free coffee. See, there's always an upside.

The Pros Weigh In: LOUIS BLACK
Cofounder of *The Austin Chronicle* and the South by Southwest (SXSW) Conferences & Festivals

• • •

The year was 1987 and Austin, Texas, was about to go from a small city of artisans and tech-heads to a leader in both fields by launching the first South by Southwest Festival. One of the men at the helm, then and now, is Louis Black, who helped build SXSW into one of the single largest social gatherings of industry professionals in the world.

The story of SXSW has become something of a legend because of people coming together who have the same things in common and want to connect. SXSW has an open-door mentality of welcoming all ideas and styles—be it in tech, music, or art—and is a perfect example of what can happen when people open their minds.

All company-sponsored activities have the same goal: to make the whole enterprise run better by bringing employees together in both day-to-day practice and in their mind-set. But it's not always that simple. Louis nailed it all those years ago, yet his philosophy is what keeps SXSW growing and successful. It is simply: "Respect other people and assume they're going to respect you." Sounds easy, but like any living, breathing organism, a group of people is a constant work in progress in which the dynamics keep changing and we have to keep up. As Louis explains:

> *Things have changed enormously. Nowadays, there are many new manners rules because of e-mail, messaging, cell phones. Communication is so much quicker. But some of the most basic rules are the ones we've operated on—sharing information, treating each other with respect, asking for feedback from people in their areas of responsibility instead of just telling them what to do. I think those things are as important now as they have ever been.*

Modern Manners Guy's 10 Tips to Survive Work-Sponsored Events

Tip #1a: The Happy Hour—Know Your Limit

Despite the occasional "case of the Mondays," work isn't always a drag. In fact, when you have good people around you, it makes a world of difference. I've had nightmare jobs where I worked with great people, which helped keep me from going insane. We've all been there, right? You have your small group of friends at work that you always hang out with (see chapter 4). And at large office events, you inevitably gravitate toward one another.

But what happens when you head out to an office happy hour with a larger group of coworkers? Specifically, with people who are outside your group? Office happy hours create camaraderie amongst the team, but can also be a dangerous breeding ground for inappropriate behavior.

I don't care if you work at the hottest bar in Las Vegas where your job is to get wild and wasted 24/7, there is always going to be a level of professionalism that even the craziest party animal shouldn't cross at a work function. I'm not trying to say you can't have fun. But acting properly at office events is not about being boring, it's about not becoming the topic of conversation at the water cooler the next day . . . or needing someone to drive you home because your face has been planted (and drooling) on the bar for an hour. Trust me, you don't want to be that person.

Everyone has their own alcohol consumption threshold and I'm sure yours is different from mine, which is why it's absolutely crucial to know your limit and, more importantly, stick to it! No matter how much fun you're having, it's still a work function and whether you like it or not, you are under the judging eyes of your colleagues, people you see every day. Some stick-in-the-mud may even report you to HR if you do something they consider inappropriate while three sheets to the wind on T.G.I. Friday's "Wings and Things" special. In addition, the last thing you need is to have that nineteen-year-old intern drive you home because all he had was bar mix and diet soda. How embarrassing!

Tip #1b: The Happy Hour—Mingle

As I mentioned before, it's great to have your small group of friends at work who are your comfort zone. However, when it comes to an office happy hour with a large group, you need to mix it up. Why limit yourself? Why not meet some great people and get to know other coworkers in a cool, relaxed environment?

While at an office happy hour, take advantage of talking to someone you rarely see. Or better yet, talk to your boss more openly. You might discover there is a real person behind that tough exterior. People tend to let their guards down at happy hours and that openness can give you the chance to interact with colleagues you usually would not have any contact with. It's also a great way to network and learn about what your coworkers are up to. Chances are, you will be pleasantly surprised about how fun someone is outside the office when they're not focused on deadlines or running to meetings. You might learn that:

- John from legal is a part-time cage fighter.
- Kristin in marketing worked as Cinderella at Disney World to pay for college.
- Simon from accounting, who makes your great-grandfather seem old, is a closet hip-hop fan.
- Paul in the tech department was once on the U.S. Ping-Pong Team.

It's limitless, I tell you. Just give it a shot. Trust me, do you know how many times I've heard "You've got to be kidding me?!" when I tell people I was a professional wrestler? I mean, I would never hide it but it's not like the topic comes up in conversation every day.

Tip #2: The Holiday Party

Similar to the office happy hour, the holiday party is the time to unwind and have some fun with your coworkers. You've worked long and hard all year and the holiday party is a celebration of your dedication to the company. Whether it's a gigantic gala at some fancy hotel, a dinner for the team at a nearby restaurant, or just pizza in the boss' office, the holiday party is the time to just be your (professional) self and wish everyone a happy and healthy New Year.

Inevitably, the holiday party tends to push the limits of our celebration style. There are always people who overindulge in the festivities. Who can blame them, right? I mean, we work hard and we're all adults, so if I want to cut loose just this once, why not?

I agree, I totally do. However, one mistake people make is thinking that just because they are outside the actual office, they are now among friends who will not judge or even remember what happened come Monday morning.

Not true.

Before you head out for the night, remember you are still at an employer-sponsored function. This can go one of two ways for you: all the way up, or so far down that you end up back to square one, having squandered any brownie points you've earned since your first day on the job (see chapter 2). Sadly, if you are the newbie, you are much more susceptible to social mishaps (and judgmental eyes) than the established employees since the old guard tend to be higher up on the ladder and have a lot more leeway. On the other hand, for the newer or middle-tier employee any big social faux pas will result in long-term consequences that you may never fully escape.

For example, in the movie *Big* Tom Hanks's character is a thirteen-year-old stuck in the body of an adult. He shows up to his company party in a ridiculous all-white tuxedo and tails, making a grand entrance on the escalator. All heads turn as he slowly emerges; people chuckle. They don't take him seriously. Luckily, the boss has a soft spot for his childlike antics.

Let me assure you: This will not be the case in real life.

Your boss will not be charmed if you show up looking like an extra in a Lady Gaga video; or if you get carted out of the building by security because you insist on using a wine bottle as your microphone while standing on top of the bar belting out "Sweet Caroline."

Eyes are all over the place, eagerly taking everything in. So instead of spending the night with Jim Beam, spend it getting to know your colleagues. Everyone's guard is down, they're not stressed, and they're eager to mingle. Take advantage of this like an adult, not like the sixteen-year-old who discovers the open bar at a wedding.

Tip #3: The Birthday Party

I'll never forget the episode of *Seinfeld* in which Elaine gets mad because every day there seems to be another birthday party or retirement event at her office and cake is being handed out constantly. She finds herself gaining weight and now dreads having to participate in workplace events. This results in her being labeled a party pooper with a bad attitude.

The people in your office are a big part of your life and when there is something to celebrate for any one of them, it's proper to drop what you're doing and join in the festivities. Sure, in *Seinfeld* it was overdramatized, but the reality is that if you added up all the minutes you actually spend celebrating your coworkers' birthdays, babies, or retirements, it's not much time at all. Don't be a bad sport. Don't schedule a meeting or call around the time of the party. We all know that it's Steve's birthday at 10:00 A.M. on Tuesday. There is no reason, unless something urgent arises, that you should miss it.

When the birthday event is in the office, bringing a gift is not required. But you'd definitely score kudos if you contribute to the party somehow. The easiest and most affordable option is to bring a tasty treat. If you can't cook or don't feel like picking out a dessert, offer to bring drinks or paper supplies (plates, napkins, paper towels, etc.). No one is expecting any gifts at all, let alone a full-blown bash. But it's always polite to contribute in some small way. Something that is fairly easy and affordable is pitching in with your colleagues for a group gift. In all my jobs, I don't think I've ever been asked to donate more than $20 for someone's birthday. It's so much better to go into the party and find a big spread, rather than stand around the conference room table singing "Happy Birthday," with not so much as a pack of Ding-Dongs to share.

Tip #4: The Office Retreat

I'm not going to sugarcoat company retreats for you—they can be a real drag. I've personally been to at least three dozen retreats of all different sizes, shapes, and vibes. Office retreats are designed to unite and educate employees.

These events tend to be off site and are designed to take your mind away from the daily grind in order to sharpen your skills and become more cohesive as a team. Some retreats are a simple day away from the office, while others are grand, expensive trips to a resort that you wish you could afford for your honeymoon. However, don't count on the latter. All that you can assume is that you'll get a break from the office for a day or so.

There are generally two types of office retreats. The first is simply a team-building exercise in which you attend a series of talks, seminars, workshops, etc. with the goal of improving employee communication or specific skills. This approach is cut and dry and you can take away what you want from it. You'll probably leave with a bunch of notes about best practices and business relationships that, if you're smart, you'll pay attention to and save. You never know when something will come up that would allow you to refer back to a lesson learned at the retreat—which would earn you substantial props from the boss. In fact, at some indeterminate moment, your boss will inevitably bring up a topic that was discussed at the retreat. And if you can't recall where you placed the materials from the event you'll regret it.

The second type of retreat has more of an earthy, crunchy, let's-talk-about-our-feelings-out-loud vibe. This tends to be awkward but is supposed to make employees more comfortable and relaxed with one another. One Modern Manners Guy Facebook friend named Joe e-mailed me about his experience at this type of retreat. His boss scheduled a company trip at a cabin in a nature preserve one hour from the city. He brought in a group therapist for the team to discuss the ups and downs of office life. The purpose was to get all the grievances on the table and, at the end of the day, to come up with a resolution for making the workplace function better. Sounds reasonable, right?

Well, not quite.

The therapist turned out to be overly friendly, overly pushy, and made things more uncomfortable rather than less. Who would have thought that employees wouldn't want to spill the beans on what bothers them about their jobs to their colleagues and boss in a log cabin?

The goal of the retreat, whether ill-planned and awkward or a rousing success, is to encourage participants to become a more cohesive team. So look at the retreat as that and only that. If you aren't into it, put on a happy face and just slog through. The worst thing you can do is draw attention to yourself by sulking or being negative. No wait, that's the second worst. The number one worst thing you can do is leave early. That's very conspicuous and no one, least of all the retreat organizers, will appreciate it.

The Pros Weigh In: BRIAN DUNCANSON
Cofounder and head of strategic planning
for the Spartan Race

• • •

In the past few years an interesting style of recreation has become popular among fitness buffs: the adventure race, in which you risk life and limb overcoming bizarre obstacles through mud, wire, walls, desert, and other unpleasant things. One of the most popular and fiercest of them all is the Spartan Race, which describes itself as "an obstacle course race designed to test your resilience, strength, stamina, quick decision-making skills, and ability to laugh in the face of adversity." I'm sorry . . . come again?

I have a hard enough time making it to my office gym one floor below my desk! And the only "laughing in the face" will be when other racers mock me for getting tangled up in mud and rope from an obstacle attempt gone wrong. However, it's this incredible exercise of will that makes the Spartan Race a bonding experience for many coworkers. And it's catching on. In the past few months, four of my friends put together teams within their companies for the Spartan Race that became their office retreat!

I mean, talk about an icebreaker, right? I can hear the boss now: "Good morning, everyone, I'm so happy you could make our retreat today. You have worked so hard that I'm rewarding you by putting you through utter torture. So without further ado . . . release the Kraken!"

But if you think about it, all of the qualities necessary for an adventure race (teamwork, challenging yourself, powering through difficulties) are also crucial for professional success in any industry. Brian Duncanson, the cofounder and chief of strategic planning for the Spartan Race, says, "There's no question that any sort of group workout will bring people closer together in their professional arena."

Brian points to the Spartan Code, which contains the tenets of the race and serves as the building ground for learning team cooperation.

- A Spartan pushes their mind and body to their limit.
- A Spartan masters their emotions.
- A Spartan learns continuously.
- A Spartan gives generously.
- A Spartan leads.
- A Spartan stands up for what they believe in, no matter the cost.
- A Spartan knows their flaws as well as they know their strengths.
- A Spartan proves themselves through actions, not words.
- A Spartan lives every day as if it were their last.

So the next time your manager mentions a potential office retreat in some lame conference room (or log cabin), suggest an adventure race as a much more intense and rewarding team-building exercise.

Now, where's that Kraken . . .

Tip #5: The Sports League

"Take me out to the ball game, take me out with the crowd, buy me some peanuts and Cracker Jacks, I don't care if I never . . . get a promotion because I just punched out the first baseman of my office softball team for crowding the base."

Office sports teams generally come in one of two distinct identities: the casual league, welcoming of any and all employees; and the win-or-die leagues with stricter recruiting practices than most cutthroat professional teams.

The first type is pretty easy to handle. If you want to play, great. If you don't or can't, it's still nice to attend a game from time to time and support your colleagues. Office sports leagues are meant to build camaraderie and, like office retreats, encourage employees to bond outside the job. Bottom line: You don't have to play to be a team player. However, this is not the case with the second type of workplace sports team.

My friend Jonathan works for a Fortune 500 company with over 2,500 employees. The company has an office softball league of 20 teams, all fighting for the coveted trophy and, of course, bragging rights. Not only does each team's captain—who is usually a manager—comb the office like a dog in heat looking for potential players, the hiring managers even go so far as to bring up the league in the job interview to gauge if the candidate had an athletic background, especially in baseball or softball. (In case you're wondering, yes, that is totally improper.) Around springtime, the team managers even recruit part-time employees from other divisions of the company to play on their teams. So when it surfaced that Jonathan played Division 1 baseball for a top-twenty team, he was not only approached right away, but was left with no choice but to participate.

Being young and new to the job, he agreed and became a standout immediately. From then on, he was treated differently. He was asked out for lunch by his manager on a regular basis. He was pulled into meetings that didn't involve him. He got all kinds of attention that had nothing to do with his job performance simply because he could hit a ball farther and run faster than anyone else at the company.

At first, this was great! He was thrilled that his baseball skills were getting him ahead. However, his fellow coworkers didn't appreciate this turn of events. Jealousies and resentments arose and strict lines formed of who was on Team Jonathan and who was not. Moreover, when he struck out for the first time, all that respect and attention from his superiors came crashing down, leaving him with zilch. Here is a case of a distinguished company putting a recreational activity above the progress and professionalism of their business.

So unless you're prepared to follow Jonathan's bad

example, don't allow anything to overshadow your work. One thing that must be made clear: The only people who get paid for their athletic ability are . . . wait for it . . . wait for it . . . *professional athletes*! So unless you work for my beloved Baltimore Orioles as their first baseman, you should not be too worried about how cutthroat the competition is in your workplace when it comes to sports. If you can throw out a guy at home from center field, well, that's just fantastic but what really matters is how you perform at your job.

I'm not saying you shouldn't participate—you should if you can—but you should not let the pressure of others who hold sports performance higher above everything else affect your career goals. Believe me, the "fame" of the guy in billing with the killer jump shot will not last as long as your success of landing that huge client. Success in the workplace is not a seasonal thing like sports. If you don't allow it to overpower your day to day, it will not become the reason why you get a paycheck.

Tip #6: The Wedding

One of the best parts about starting a new job is meeting new people. And as I've said before, your colleagues can become an extended family, complete with the same perks of an actual family, like being invited to social events. I have been to at least a dozen weddings of people I've met at work. Being invited to a coworker's wedding is an honor. When this happens, what they're saying is that not only do they respect you as a coworker, they appreciate you as a friend with whom they want to share one of the biggest moments in their life. As you can imagine, not everyone from the office will be invited and that is where this momentous occasion can become a sticky situation.

If you work in a medium- to large-sized company, you have to assume that you are one of the select few to receive an invitation to the wedding. As such, it's best to limit your discussion of it to the inner circle of those who will be attending. You don't want anyone to feel jealous (which they will) or upset (which they also will) at not being invited.

Secondly, when going to a coworker's wedding, unless you're actually in the wedding party it's improper to make demands. By this, I mean the question of bringing a date. Here's my rule when it comes to dates at weddings: unless you are living together, engaged, or married, that special someone is not guaranteed a seat at the table. If your current significant other doesn't fit this category and your colleague doesn't grant you a "plus one" on the invitation, then you'll have to make do alone for the four hours that day. Weddings are expensive, so just because you are truly in love with Mr./Ms. Perfect whom you just met last month, it doesn't mean you should insist they be invited.

If you start to argue with a coworker about their wedding, it will inevitably lead to conflict in the workplace, which will be detrimental to you both. Save arguing over dates and guests for the bride's and groom's families. They'll love it. The only request you can make is about dietary restrictions, such as if you're a vegetarian or keep kosher. Otherwise, bring a gift, smile, dance, and wish the couple well. Or, if you're too disgruntled about not being able to bring Mr./Ms. Perfect and can't fathom four or five hours by your lonesome, then provide a suitable excuse and decline the invitation.

Tip #7: The Wedding Shower

The big day is right around the corner and everyone in the office is getting together to show their enthusiasm for a colleague who is getting hitched. Here's what usually happens: It'll be a surprise, you will deck out an office or their cube with decorations, everyone will bring in a treat or two, and gifts will be given. This is pretty standard across the board. I'm not saying you have to do any of these—but you should do at least some. I mean, it's a wedding! It's a beautiful time in someone's life, you can spare a lunch hour or a break in the day to congratulate them.

If the organizer has designated that the wedding shower is a surprise, don't be the stick-in-the-mud that ruins it. If surprises aren't your thing, don't volunteer to be on the team responsible for distracting the bride or groom from finding out about the party. Too many things can go wrong. And when it's a surprise, do not put on your calendar "Christina's Surprise Wedding Shower!" I'm sure I don't need to explain why this would be a bad idea.

Regarding gifts, this isn't the time to break the bank, especially if you are invited to the wedding since you're already bringing a gift to the main event. For the office wedding shower, I recommend pitching in for a group gift because this allows the bride or groom to get something rather pricey that most people would not buy on their own, but in a group, when everyone pitches in, it's much more affordable. And always stick to the registry. Never guess on a gift. This is the beauty and purpose of the registry. Use it.

Lastly, if you aren't friendly with the person or are sour about not being invited to the wedding, you should still attend the shower. Why? Because it's polite to show respect for your fellow coworkers on such a joyous occasion. Not enough of a reason? OK fine, how about this: Most people in the office will attend the party. So if there are twenty-five employees and only twenty-four show up, you stand out as a self-absorbed grinch. The boss will likely be there and your absence will be noted. If you truly can't stand the person, just don't contribute as much (or anything) to the group gift. There, sourpuss, you have a small victory. Enjoy.

Tip #8: The Baby Shower

A close cousin to the wedding shower is the baby shower. It has similar rules to the wedding shower: it's usually a surprise (which I always find weird—why would you surprise a pregnant woman who is in an emotional and fragile state?), you should always attend, and gifts are required.

By the way, since it's the 21st century, a baby shower is no longer solely for women. When my wife was expecting, my colleagues surprised me with an awesome shower in the office. However, for the most part, a baby shower tends to be for a woman and this can be a breeding ground for potential mishaps.

When you become a parent, you join a club of people in which talking about body parts and bodily functions is about as casual as talking about the weather. "Ugh, the other day, I was in the middle of Target and Noah pooped all over my hand. What was I to do?" If this was college and you just told your classmates this happened to you, you'd never hear the end of it. But as a parent, it's all part of the game. So people feel more open in sharing stories about bodies and babies and expect you not to mind. But this type of sharing is only meant for close friends, not coworkers. Sure, you're friendly, but if you ask your pregnant female colleague if her breasts are sore, I feel it's only proper to be slapped. I don't advocate violence, but unless you're a doctor this is off limits. I've actually witnessed a fifty-something male coworker ask this exact question. I thought the poor woman was going to fall through the ground in embarrassment.

A similar but far more humiliating thing happened to my friend Bethany, who worked for a very popular high-end magazine in Manhattan. At her baby shower, her seventy-five-year-old (male) boss decided to stand up and address the room with a toast for Bethany. The entire staff of forty or so was in attendance to witness this guy go on and on about how wonderful it has been to watch Bethany's body blossom. "Bethany had a great body before she was pregnant and it's been an amazing experience to watch her transform into the fecund female form that it is today."

No matter how many people coughed nervously or cleared their throats, or how red Bethany's face got, nothing could deter this guy from his celebratory ode to her figure. It was a profoundly uncomfortable, cringe-worthy experience for everyone (except the clueless old toaster). Guess what happened next? Bethany marched straight to HR and filed a complaint. If it wasn't for her baby's early arrival the following week, this could have easily gone to litigation.

"What? Come on, we're all thinking it!"

Okay, folks, not that I even need to say it, but it is hugely, *massively* improper to talk about anyone's body in the workplace, especially in front of other coworkers, and even more especially, about a pregnant woman. Bethany was well aware of her body changing and I'm sure she knew that everyone took notice, but as any woman will attest, they don't want it pointed out . . . let alone at work . . . in front of everybody . . . by their boss! What was he thinking?

Tip #9: The Conference

Here's a fact: You will probably go to so many conferences in your career that they will blur together like an endless guitar solo at a Phish concert. However, conferences are a great opportunity to learn new skills and network with others in your field. Even if the conference you're going to is a snooze-fest, there are still many perks to attending.

The best way to handle a conference is to be selective when choosing which to attend and then cooperative when your boss makes you go to one you're not interested in. The latter will give you leverage for the former. For example, if your boss makes you go to a dullsville conference and then you find out about one that you're dying to attend, speak up (and tacitly remind your boss that you went to that other boring one for him). You will have to make a case for why you should go and provide good reasons. If the event is totally outside the scope of your job, it's going to be a tough sell. But if you get innovative and look for interesting conferences that are affordable and applicable to your field, they can be great opportunities to meet and mingle with big players in your industry.

Conferences come with strings attached. Don't treat a conference like a free ticket to endless cups of coffee and cheese Danishes. When you attend a conference, your boss is shelling out dollars to secure your spot and they'll expect you to come back with more than just a bag full of free swag. When you return, expect questions like "How was it? What did you learn? Who did you talk to?" and you better have an intelligent response. If you come back to the office saying that you didn't learn anything worthwhile and didn't talk to anyone important, your boss will take that as arrogance and consider you a waste of money. No matter how boring or tedious the conference, you can (and should) always learn something that you can apply to your job.

Bottom line on conferences: Meet people, be friendly, take notes—don't just cower in the corner like a freshman at a high school dance.

And, of course, enjoy the freebies!

> Networking, both externally and within your company, is the best way to get ahead in the corporate world. Still looking for a job? Start volunteering for organizations in the industry that you want to get involved with.
> —Tim McDonald, community manager
> at Huffington Post Live

Tip# 10: Meeting Cancelation Etiquette

Throughout your career, you'll have to cancel a meeting that has been on your calendar for a while. Whether you legitimately can't make it due to some unforeseen circumstance, or you simply just want to ditch it for a better event, you will be tasked with messaging the other attendees to explain yourself.

We're all human and things come up that are outside of our control, so canceling meetings is just a part of life. People usually won't hold it against you, as long as you're not a repeat offender. But that doesn't mean you get off the hook so easily. When you do cancel, you have to make sure the other party knows where you're coming from and that you're duly apologetic for wasting their time.

Let's look at two scenarios:

Scenario 1: Circumstances outside your control. A traffic jam, a public transportation breakdown, a babysitter gone MIA, or any other event over which you haven't the slightest control all fall into this category. This scenario is the most frustrating because when something happens to make you late, you feel helpless. So you stare at your watch miserably as time gets away from you, knowing that Paris Hilton has a better chance of winning *Celebrity Jeopardy* than you do of making your meeting.

The Resolution: When this happens, there are three steps to take. First and foremost, apologize profusely. Secondly, reschedule right away. Make sure they understand that you will open up your schedule to work around theirs because the cancelation was your fault. This is not a fun situation, but you have to swallow your pride, accept that you have inconvenienced someone, and work to make it right.

Thirdly, make up for your cancelation by making your next meeting as pleasant as possible for the other party. If you are meeting for coffee, buy them a cup. If you are going to lunch, pick up the bill. If you are supposed to meet at your office, have fresh bottled water, coffee, or snacks ready. These are little things that will go a long way to make amends.

Scenario 2: You're ditching them. OK, I'll be the first to stand up and admit it—I've canceled with someone because I just didn't want to meet with them. It's not a regular habit and I do feel badly about it after the fact, but sometimes you just don't feel like chatting, presenting, or hearing someone's wacky idea about how bringing back the VCR is going to be the next big hipster "movement." Whatever the reason, if you're going to lie, you have to cover your ass. What do I mean? Well, let's meet my friend David to better illustrate this point.

David, an attorney in San Diego, often consults with start-ups on contractual issues related to new project launches. On one occasion he promised his cousin that he would help him out with a new idea, but kept postponing the meeting because he thought the idea was stupid. He figured this cousin would take a hint and find another lawyer, but nope, he kept at David.

One day, they were supposed to meet up yet again, but David bailed at the last minute. He told his cousin that he had a terrible day at work and had an urgent client meeting, but instead David was in Napa Valley for the weekend. There was no urgent client, only a 1995 merlot and a new girlfriend by his side.

While out at dinner, his girlfriend snapped some photos and posted them on Facebook. Well, as the world of social media goes, David was tagged in the photo and it of course appeared on his news feed (see chapter 5). Guess who was one of David's 1,200 friends who saw it? That's right, his cousin, who commented, "That looks like a really urgent meeting to me . . ." Busted! I can't even describe to you the wrath that fell upon David from his family.

The Resolution: You've either purposely or accidently proven that you're a total twit by getting caught doing something other than keeping your promise to meet. Congrats! The only way to fix it is to apologize. Profusely. After that you have to grovel for another chance. Yes, the tables have turned and you are the one requesting the meeting.

Whether cousin or colleague, you should always keep in mind that your reputation is on the line. After you've apologized, send a gift to make amends and ask to start over. What type of gift? Well, that depends on the person, the situation, and the level of jerkiness you reached. For example, when David told me what he did, I thought an expensive bottle of wine was in order. So he purchased a rare vintage and attached a handwritten letter. (NOTE: Handwritten always shows more care and thought than a typed letter or e-mail.) The letter read, "Sorry for being a jerk. I feel guilty but just needed to get away for a few days. Please don't hate me. I hope this bottle will show you how I sorry I am. Give me another chance, please." He shipped it out next day. Double kiss-ass points here!

MODERN MANNERS GUY QUIZ

It's your office happy hour and everyone is throwing back shots and having a good time. You generally don't drink, but the boss keeps egging you on to have a glass and join the party. What do you do?

A Honestly tell your boss and coworkers that you're not a big drinker and you'd rather stick to soda.

B Say, "Eh, when in Rome . . ." and despite your low alcohol tolerance, start drinking to keep up with your colleagues while secretly wondering how—or if—you'll get home.

C Lie. Tell them you're taking medication for your back, tennis elbow, toothache, eyebrow piercing, whatever, so it's probably best if you don't mix it with alcohol.

D Leave in disgust because you can't believe you work with such arrogant bullies who would force others to drink.

Answer

Trick question. It's either **A** or **C**, depending on the dynamics of your workplace. Let me first say that I tend to lean on the side of honesty, but sometimes lying is the best medicine. If you know that the truth may be mocked or would make you seem like a stodgy square, then a white lie that doesn't hurt anyone is the way to go.

However, as I said, honesty is usually the best approach. You may get some odd looks or ignorant responses, but this isn't high school. If you don't drink, don't. If you don't like taking smoke breaks, why should you? And you only have to say it once because if you make your point clearly, succinctly, and without leaving any unanswered questions, it will be the last time you have to deal with it.

A note to the ladies: If you are at an office event that involves drinking and you decline alcohol, it is very likely that people will assume you're pregnant. If you are pregnant and don't want to share that info just yet, or if you simply don't want to drink, option C is your best bet. "I'm taking medication for lower lumbar pain and can't mix it with alcohol" isn't exciting enough to invite further questions.

MODERN MANNERS GUY'S
WORK EVENTS TOOL KIT

1 **PACK GREETING CARDS.** Keep a pack of generic, nondenominational, congratulatory greeting cards at your desk so when a colleague's birthday/retirement/baby shower/wedding/whatever arises, you can quickly scribble a note and have something to show them that you're happy for their big event.

2 **STICK TO THE REGISTRY.** Wedding and shower registries are polarizing—some think they're great while others find them unoriginal and unexciting because they take all the surprise out of gift giving. Me? I think registries are the best thing since the open bar. People tell you what they want and you get it for them. Brilliant! It takes all the stress out of gift buying. So when you attend a wedding or a shower, stick to the registry. It's there for a reason. They want what's on the list. No need to worry about wowing them when they've already picked out the perfect gift.

3 **YOU DON'T HAVE TO BE AN ALL-STAR TO SCORE.** Office sports can get out of hand with the pressure to win big. But not everyone is good at sports, or as good as they used to be. However, this shouldn't keep you from joining in the league. So what if you can't slam dunk or hit a home run? You can still keep stats, manage players, organize the happy hours after the games, or help out with refreshments and equipment at the game. Sports games are designed to get coworkers to interact, so there's no reason you can't find some way to be a part of the team.

SEVEN

Business Travel Etiquette

Planes, trains, and automobiles are the fastest way down the corporate ladder.

> If you're in "every man for himself" mode while traveling, it tells me a lot about you as a person. You're not a team player. You're not thinking about the big picture.
> —Ken Austin, cofounder of Marquis Jet and founder/chairman of Tequila Avión

Unlike decades ago, when traveling was considered a luxury, today's common travel experience is more like a trip to the DMV, or like having your teeth pulled without Novocain, or like the tragic news that Honey Boo Boo was featured on Barbara Walters's list of Most Fascinating People of 2012 (I'm not kidding!).

Nowadays, the difficulties and frustrations of travel can test even the patience of Mother Teresa. However, all the unpleasant aspects of travel can quickly be resolved with a little understanding and a lot of goodwill. (Right, because that's soooo easy.) Make peace with the fact that unless you own your own airline, a fleet of buses, or a private railroad company, you'll have to travel like everyone else and endure all the *un*pleasantries that come with it.

In the classic movie *Planes, Trains and Automobiles,* John Candy and Steve Martin are forced to endure each other's differences while taking every means of transportation en route to Thanksgiving dinner. They nearly kill each other because of John Candy's obnoxious, unmannerly behavior. I think of that movie every time I travel. From loud talking, to odd eating habits, to drunken escapades, to nasty hygiene, it's as if being on the road brings out our dark side.

Regardless of where you work or what industry you're in, you'll probably have to do some traveling for your job. Whether it's a ten-minute metro ride, a twenty-mile drive to a neighboring city, or even a cross-country or international flight, traveling for work could very well be the Olympics of manners. And like any Olympian, you can't let obstacles that are placed in front of you get in the way of scoring a gold medal. So with that, let's make sure our bags are secure in our overhead compartments and take a wild ride of travel etiquette. *DING!*

"Oops, my bad. I left my cell phone in my pocket."

The Pros Weigh In: KEN AUSTIN
Cofounder of Marquis Jet and
founder/chairman of Tequila Avión

• • •

When it came to the topic of business travel, I decided to reach out to someone who revolutionized the travel industry. Ken Austin is the cofounder of Marquis Jet, a private airline company. He's also the chairman and founder of Tequila Avión (which you may remember from *Entourage*).

Ken is the kind of guy who will fly on a whim from New York to London and back in a single day just for a lunch meeting. He's also the kind of guy who chased his dream of creating his own premier tequila company. "I literally, sight unseen, got on a plane and went to Mexico. I flew to Jalisco to figure out if I could find a distillery that would let me do what I wanted to do. I wanted to create the greatest tequila in the world, using the best ingredients." So, needless to say, Ken has unique insight into the world of business travel.

> *When people go into an airport, it's amazing to watch personalities change. It's almost like the frenzy after Hurricane Sandy in New York when people were rationing gasoline and created a mass panic because they had to go get another quarter tank of gas so they could keep their tank at full. That's what created the shortage—people were hoarding. And it's the same thing with airports. People start to panic and act irrationally. "Oh, I'm going to miss my flight!" Or, "I have to get in line!" . . . even when it's not time to get in line.*

I know what you're thinking: "Come on, this guy can fly around the globe in his own fleet of jets! He has no idea what it's *really* like to travel like the rest of us." Well, my friends, you would be right . . . and wrong. Yes, Ken created a luxury travel industry basically because the standard way of flying was (as he said above) too chaotic. However, Ken Austin could very well be the most down-to-earth aviation leader that ever existed. Don't believe me? Turns out that the onetime King of the Skies flies . . . coach.

The way I was raised—and I can't say I'm perfect—but I really do believe in showing respect for everyone around you. I don't care who they are. When you're traveling with someone and they become one of those rats in the race . . . it's a test of your patience. The stress of traveling commercially is what made Marquis Jet so successful. When you travel, you see people's real personalities come out. And you can judge if this is the kind of person you want to spend time with. If they're not nice to the flight attendant, to the person taking your bag, to other passengers, well, then you know something about their real character.

Ken is right. If you've ever flown, you've seen people who forget the world around them and only focus on what *they* have to do and where *they* have to go. Who hasn't been mowed down by a crazed traveler running through the airport as if Godzilla was chasing them because they overslept and were late to the gate? When you make everyone around you bend to your wishes, it shows an incredible lack of professionalism and maturity. This is doubly true when you travel for business because you will inevitably travel with colleagues or bosses who will get to see your true stripes and likely extrapolate on what that says about you as a whole.

Modern Manners Guy's Top 10 Tips for Business Travel Etiquette

Tip #1: Pack Light

In the 2009 film *Up in the Air,* George Clooney plays a veteran corporate traveler who spends more days in flight every year than on the ground. When a young co-worker (Anna Kendrick) joins him for a trip, she gets a blunt lesson in professional packing. Kendrick's character arrives in the airport lugging what appears to be a suitcase from the 1970s that could hold enough clothes for a family of twelve. Clooney's character shakes his head in disgust and then makes her buy a new, reasonably sized carry-on, which she must repack in the middle of the airport. Kendrick's character illustrates a common rookie mistake.

When you get a job that involves travel, the first thing I recommend is to invest in appropriate luggage. Your college backpack with the ripped straps does not scream, "I'm a professional." Instead, it says, "I'm still in college and my mom bought me this bag." Having proper luggage is like dressing for the job interview (see chapter 1). You want to look the part from head to toe, including accessories. This does not have to be a costly investment, either. You do not need top-of-the line, Louis Vuitton taiga leather, just something that rolls easily and is light, but also durable. Trust me, you'll be doing a lot of lifting and

pulling so you want it to hold up. If you need help deciding on what to get, just ask a colleague who travels a lot.
They'll have plenty of suggestions.

Now that you have the appropriate luggage, what to
put in it? Business travel packing means traveling light,
small, efficient, and not padding your bag with items for
every possible scenario. If you're going to Phoenix in June,
you may surely come across a slightly cooler night that
dips below 80 degrees, but packing a bulky jacket for that
trip is a waste of valuable space. Even though it's nice to
have options for every possible event (networking, drinks,
dinner with colleagues or clients, etc.), be realistic about
how many changes of clothes you need to pack. Do you
really need seven options for a weekend? Really? Lastly,
make sure to bring pieces that are versatile enough to mix
and match for any occasion. For example, a suit and a few
shirts can create a numbers of different outfits, from business casual to formal.

Tip #2: What to Wear?

As I discussed in chapter 1, dressing for the role you
want to play at work will cause others to perceive you in
that role. The same thing applies to dressing for travel
(although, I'm not saying to dress like the TSA agent—
that will never go over well). What I am saying is that you
should dress specifically for the type of travel you're doing
that day. I've found that when you dress ready to maneuver through the security line (bonus points if you can

undress quickly), you'd be surprised how much smoother the experience can be.

Oftentimes when traveling for work, you have to go to a meeting right away after landing at your destination. With business trips, you usually dress for the upcoming meeting. With family vacations, you usually dress ready to go to your hotel as soon as you land. And even with the romantic getaway, you may dress ready for a fun night out. No matter which it is, I recommend dressing to make it through the security line first and worrying about what you'll be wearing when you land second. Yes, you can wear loads of jewelry, high heels with many metallic straps, and carry everything you need in your pocket. But that won't do you any favors when you're stuck in the security checkpoint for twenty minutes removing everything and getting a cavity search because some piece of metal in your outfit is making the machine go bananas. This will undoubtedly annoy everyone behind you and they won't be shy about making their impatience heard. So wear simple, security-friendly clothing and pack whatever you need in your carry-on so you can change after you get through the line.

When you travel for work, remember that you are still representing your company, so your favorite shirt that says "Who Farted?" may—call me crazy—not be a good idea to wear on the plane.

Tip #3: Road Trip!

In my first job after college, I and two other coworkers took a trip from Washington, D.C., to Pennsylvania, a three-hour drive each way if we didn't hit traffic (which we did, of course). The best part was that I liked my coworkers, which always helps, but the worst part is that road trips never quite go as planned. There are too many variables—especially traffic—that you can't account for. But even with rain, sleet, road closures, or smelly riders, there are some things you can do to make a road trip with colleagues tolerable, even fun!

For starters, determine ahead of time who will be driving and, if you take turns, who will drive when so that there are no disagreements along the way. Also, decide on a solid time and place of the departure and stick to it. After all, you have known about this trip for a while and everyone has had time to adjust their schedules. You don't want to show up to the departure point an hour late because you had something else to take care of. If your colleagues are coming to pick you up, don't start packing your bag when you hear the doorbell ring. Being on time and being considerate of others is simply professional. Anything less is not.

Along with splitting the driving responsibilities, you also want to split the cost for gas. Gas prices nowadays make a night out at the finest steakhouse seem like a Happy Meal at McDonald's. So when someone offers to drive, be respectful and pitch in for gas. There is no reason why someone should have to not only drive, but also take on the gas bill as well. Even if they arrived to your house with a full tank, I always insist on contributing $10 or $20 toward gas money. And if they won't take it, leave it in their cup holder on the sly. (This is a moot point if your employer is picking up the tab for gas.)

When you are sharing the ride with someone, you must always remember to be a good passenger. What is a good passenger? Well, along with not insisting that everyone listen to your music, or not eating a super-smelly sandwich that makes everyone gag, you should remember that the person driving is not your chauffeur. When I was a pro wrestler, one of the codes my team followed was that we couldn't all fall asleep in the car when traveling to a match, leaving one guy to drive alone. This is a rule that most pro wrestlers follow and when you don't, you'll feel it in the ring later on. I've actually witnessed a veteran wrestler lay a full-on smackdown on a rookie who not only nodded off as soon as his rear end hit the seat, but didn't even offer to take a shift for the four-hour drive. Last time he did that!

I understand that if you're driving for many hours, you may have to sleep. But don't bail on the driver right away. Be helpful with directions, check their blind spots, and most importantly, just keep them company during the ride. Colleagues will remember you for being a team player both in and out of the office, and this is an easy way to make a good impression—as a bonus, being an alert and engaged passenger is a great way to get to know your colleagues and learn more about the dynamics of the company.

Tip #4: Airport Security

I will openly admit that my initial reason for writing on this topic was to shout my grievances to the world about how much I dislike the security line at airports. However, I need to keep a more neutral stance and concede that there are always two sides to every story. I mean, after all, maybe I'm wrong that the security line should move faster? Maybe we *should* get full-body searches as if we're all smuggling illegal substances? And maybe that elderly couple that can hardly walk, let alone assault someone, *is* a danger to fellow passengers? Who knows, right? Thankfully, when it comes to airport security etiquette, we can be a part of the solution.

Unless you enjoy being probed like in an alien abduction, you have to learn how to maneuver airport security with minimal, ahem, penetration. The easiest way is to show up early. Simple, right? But being early to airports will ensure that you get through the security line in a reasonable amount of time *and* make your flight. After all, the airlines wait for no one. They don't care if you are just a minute late or if you got held up for an hour because your Great-aunt Trudy's wheelchair had to be screened for bombs. The plane has to leave on time. I respect that. No one wants to be the reason a plane is delayed—it's a nightmare domino effect—so arriving to the airport early is the best way to make sure everyone has a smooth transition through the security line.

Arriving within two hours of departure is key. Too much time? Some would say so, but I will say it's a heck of a lot easier to arrive early to the airport than get there and see the security line is wrapped around the perimeter of the entire airport. I once traveled during Christmas (a bad idea, I know) and it felt as though I was in the line for a free iPad or something. If we all arrived early, the security lines would move more efficiently because they do adjust for people who arrive late. You know those people, they get to go ahead of everyone like they're so special when really the airport security doesn't want them to hold up the airplane from leaving on time. I can't stand when that happens.

The second way to get through the process unscathed is to accept that the airline security process is rough. The line will be annoying, people will be mad, they will be in a hurry, and they will complain. Kids will cry, teenagers will be texting, and the snooty first-class flier will refuse to get off his Crackberry. It's like road trips (see Tip #3): you can leave early, you can be fully gassed up, but one person talking on their cell phone who rear-ends the car in front of them can ruin it for us all.

Air travel is not glamorous and the security line is the epitome of frustrating. More often than not, people will be unfriendly—whether it's fellow passengers or the unsmiling FAA drones looking at your ID card as if you are one of America's Most Wanted. Sometimes I think that if they had a bar *before* the security line, rather than *after,* it could save a lot of aggravation and make the whole process much more tolerable.

There are no surprises here, no velvet ropes to sneak under, the security staff are not your friends and, frankly, couldn't care less if you have an enjoyable trip. Their job is about safety. So, expecting comfortable, special treatment is a colossal waste of time. Take a Zen approach to the security line and realize patience is a virtue . . . Namaste.

Tip #5: On the Plane (Part 1)

Long gone are the days when airlines focused on spoiling their customers. My dad used to tell me about the olden days (aka, the 1970s) when getting on an airplane felt like you were a celebrity with people waiting on you hand and foot. Now, they even throw celebrities off the plane! So, unless you're Sir Richard Branson or Jay-Z and can fly on your own private jet, you'll likely encounter the gambit of foul manners, foul odors, and foul food en route to your destination. It's a nightmare. The seats are too small, the air is stale, babies are crying, and everyone wants to get off as soon as possible. Which is why accepting this new status quo is the easiest way to get through your flight.

It's like an awkward blind date that you wished never happened. The only way to get through it is to relax, stay focused, and try to make the best of the situation. They say that high expectations are the quickest way to disappointment, and air travel is a great example of this. Don't expect a gourmet meal—realize you will get a 100-calorie pack of chips, a Dixie cup–sized, watered-down soda, and (if you're lucky) a napkin the size of a business card. Don't expect the person sitting next to you to smell like roses or mind his own business—chances are they will reek of cigarettes and one too many airport lounge drinks.

Lastly, but perhaps most importantly, don't expect manners. So, when you find yourself about to rip your hair out because the person next to you will not stop talking, sit back, put your headphones on, and just think about the soft landing to come.

Tip #6: On the Plane (Part 2)

Apparently there is a misconception on what comes with purchasing your airplane ticket. Allow me to clarify: The *only* thing that's included in the purchase price is the fart-stained seat. Oh, and a bag of stale crackers that wouldn't even fill a toddler's palm. If you're lucky, *maybe* you'll get your choice of an aisle or window. But that's about it.

My wife will be the first one to tell you that I fall asleep on planes, even before takeoff. She'll probably also tell you that I snore. Guilty. However, whether you snore, twitch, or sing show tunes in your sleep, one thing remains constant: the seat is not a bed (and neither is the seat next to you). And don't get me started on the rules of the arm-rest. How many times have you had to sit next to someone, watch them falling asleep, and next thing you know, they're planted facedown on your tray?

I'm not saying that you can't sleep on a plane. But if you're going to nap, the proper way to catch some Zs is to remain in your area. Don't lounge over anyone else, don't hog the armrest like a football, and don't rest your head on a stranger's shoulder. If you know for sure you are going to fall asleep ahead of time, try to get a seat by the window. This way, you have something to lean against that's not going to resent you. If you are unfortunate enough to have someone else designate you as their new pillow, the proper thing to do is to wake them and let them know they are in your space. There is nothing wrong or unmannerly about doing this. Don't rattle, shake, or otherwise manhandle them—just kindly tap them and ask them to please remain in their area.

The Pros Weigh In: LYNDON and JAMIE CORMACK
Founders of Herschel Supply Co.

• • •

No matter where or how you travel, you can't go anywhere without the right bags to hold your life's necessities. Brothers Lyndon and Jamie Cormack, founders of Herschel Supply Co., have been making travel a much more fashionable endeavor since 2009. The Brothers Cormack have traveled across the globe for their company, oftentimes accompanied by their employees, and I wanted to find out how they handle the blurring boundaries of traveling with colleagues or bosses. So I asked them: Are you still "on the clock" while traveling with coworkers, or can you relax once you are on the plane, train, or in the car? Lyndon responded:

> *This will depend on the relationship you have with your colleagues or boss. Every situation is different and there is no blanket answer to cover every scenario. For example, at Herschel Supply Co., work is always on our mind, but it doesn't mean we are on the clock 24/7. I take pride in letting our employees let their hair down and to be off the clock to a certain degree. In other environments, being "on the clock" may mean holding back the temptation to party or to speak casually. The most important thing is to accurately judge what is expected. If you feel that something may be inappropriate, then leave it for when you're with your true friends.*

Because the Herschel Supply Co. is beloved all over the world, the Cormack brothers have encountered a lot of new cultures and beliefs during their travels. In business, especially in this constantly shrinking world, it's inevitable that you will meet people who are not just like you, or don't believe the same things you do. So when you enter a new environment, keep an open mind:

> *Do research, read, and find out what to expect. There are many resources out there right now*

that can help a person prepare for international encounters. Of course the best way is to visit these countries before going there for business, but that is not a necessary investment. A little preparation can go a long way toward smoothing over any culture clash.

I visited Armenia to research a famous filmmaker and to create some of my own work. The first night I was feasting with colleagues and we were served delicious homemade fig vodka. I naturally drank some of it while eating. Turns out, this is a sign of great disrespect! You're supposed to drink only when everyone else at the table drinks during a toast. Luckily, they didn't take offense and taught me the correct way to drink in Armenia, which is collectively in unison.

—Jonathan Monaghan, world-renowned artist and animator

Tip #7: Train Travel

The other day, I got a text from my buddy Jason saying, "I'm on the train right now and you HAVE to do a Modern Manners Guy episode about train etiquette—it's like a freak show in here!" That was his first text. The others—which arrived about every five minutes—not only cracked me up, but reminded me of how interesting train travel can be.

I don't know why, but there's something about traveling by train that makes people want to have loud, private phone conversations, regardless of who is around them.

I mean, at least when a person screams on their phone in a supermarket or a retail store, you can walk down a different aisle or go outside to escape. But on a train, you're trapped— oftentimes in close proximity. When you're faced with this sort of rudeness, I'd ordinarily advise you to stand up and take mannerly action . . . unless you're on the train.

When someone is so inconsiderate that they lose track of where they are, what they're doing, and who is watching or hearing them, there is nothing you can do to contain it. If someone is so loud (and possibly angry) on the phone, you don't want to confront them. It's best to simply move to another seat or, if you can't, try focusing really hard on your book or your phone like it contains the secret of life. The last thing you want to do is politely approach the person only to have him or her lash out at you and create an unfortunate confrontation.

Another unfortunate situation when riding the rails is who will sit next to you. Take my routine trips from Baltimore to New York. It's not that far a distance, yet it includes ten stops, which means ten new sets of people coming and going onto the train. And one of the rudest things I witness is oblivious passengers not offering up their seats to people who need it more. I can't tell you how many times I've been on a train and watched a heavily pregnant woman or an elderly person stand while others sit and watch. I mean, what has the world come to? It's even worse when able-bodied people are sitting in those seats reserved for the disabled and they still don't get up.

If you witness such poor behavior, you can simply say, "I'm sorry, but I think you are sitting in the seats reserved for someone who may need it." They will hopefully get the hint and get up off their lazy ass.

Tip #8: The Corporate Credit Card

I'll never forget receiving my first credit card from my parents. I was in college and thought that the $2,000 limit was like hitting the lottery. *Lunch?* Swipe. *A new sweatshirt?* Swipe it again. *Treating the girls that were only hanging out with me and my friends because we were buying drinks?* Go right ahead, barkeep, just charge it.

(In case you're wondering, nothing panned out with the girls at the bar. Apparently being able to sneak into a college bar at eighteen does not mean you, in fact, have "game." That, and the actual twenty-one-year-olds who came over shortly after I unloaded $75 worth of shots were apparently more attractive than me and my pimple-faced friends. Go figure.)

Their loss was Visa's gain because it never occurred to me that I actually had to pay the charges back, let alone that my mom would see what I bought. That was the worst part! How do you explain $135 at Taco Bell in one week? I couldn't. Needless to say, my first year at college was a very interesting lesson in personal finance. So when you get a corporate card from your employer, think of it as a "For Emergencies Only" safety net, to be used judiciously.

Oftentimes, your boss will tell you to treat clients or

"Yeah, front desk, I'm going to need another round of lobster tails, ASAP. Yup, just put it on the company card . . . Wait . . . bring up a dessert menu, too."

colleagues as necessary and set a budget for you. But if he doesn't, always ask what your monthly limit is so you aren't hit with any surprises. Also, some companies have strict limits for how and where their corporate cards can be used. For example, I had a government employee credit card that had a limit of what I could spend each day, along with how I could spend it. When I tried to buy a bag of pretzels, a soda, and a magazine in an airport kiosk, it was denied. I called the credit card company and was told that the card was not to be used for certain vendors. I had no idea.

What if I took clients to a dinner and the restaurant was not on the list of approved vendors and the card was declined? It would have been incredibly humiliating.

When you use a company card, it's not a free ride. You may be allowed to "treat" others for business purposes, but every charge is on record and everything has stipulations. You have to keep receipts of all purchases because you will probably have to submit those to the accounting department every month. Even if that's not required, always do it anyway. You never know when there will be an error. If you keep everything on hand and organized—when others didn't—you will look like the responsible employee.

Tip #9: Hotel Etiquette

My colleague Nick and I recently had to fly from Baltimore to Minneapolis for business. Tell me why it takes two layovers and eleven hours to go 940 miles? Why do I have to travel from Baltimore to Atlanta, to Ohio, and then to Minneapolis? I'm no geography buff, but I'm pretty sure that's not the fastest route. Given this ridiculous itinerary, you can imagine how thrilled I was to finally arrive at my hotel room.

I have to say, I love hotels. And when you stay in a nice one you can't help but get caught up in all the comforts. In the hospitality industry, it's their job to do whatever is necessary to win you over. So when Nick got upgraded from a standard room to a suite because the room he reserved was not ready, he was thrilled. He couldn't sleep, so he ordered a movie. Then he discovered the fridge stocked with beverages. "Why not have a few . . . or fifteen?" he thought. They're so small, how can you have just one? Oh, and room service? Don't mind if I do. I mean, that steak for $50 *has* to be delicious. He was so caught up in the hotel's offerings that he nearly fell over when the bill was presented to him at the end of our stay. Sure, he got a great room with a view at a sweet rate, but all those little extras added up and his trip ended up costing him as much as a flight from New York to Paris. Ouch!

So when you're staying at a hotel, especially if it's on the company dime, remember that virtually nothing is free. If it looks too good to be true, it likely is. And nothing is really yours. The robe is just a rental. The towels are only for use while you're there. And those drinks are the opposite of complementary.

Next time you stay at a hotel for work, make sure to ask what is included in the room rate. Is there a fee for WiFi? What about breakfast? Laundry? Some things may be free, but never assume. After all, you know what happens if you assume, right? That's right . . . you end up spending up the wazoo for treating the hotel room like a scene from *The Hangover*. Oh, and of course, you make an ass out of you and me.

Tip #10: Drinking While Traveling

Last year, on a train ride home from New York, I was sitting in the food car having a sandwich and working on my next Modern Manners Guy column. A gentleman in a fine business suit sat across from me. He was traveling with a younger colleague and before the train even pulled out of the station, he downed two small bottles of wine. I kid you not! Now, everyone's tolerance is different—mine is about the same as it was in high school when I got drunk on leftover Manischewitz—so I don't immediately judge a person by what and how much they drink. But within ten minutes of downing the bottles, the wine took its effect and this previously polished professional became more and more incoherent.

As the ride went on, he continued drinking. Soon, the jacket came off and the knot in his tie was loosened. Two hours later, his hair was disheveled, his eyes were droopy, and he drooled as he babbled nonsense about marketing reports (or was it "making his mark"? I couldn't tell). I was embarrassed for him and I'm pretty sure his young colleague was as well. He typed away on his laptop furiously, trying to divert his eyes from his drunken coworker who kept pushing the young colleague to "Drink up! Quit bein' such a stiff!" Impressively, the younger colleague handled this unpleasant situation quite well, but it was clear he couldn't wait for the ride to be over.

This was a lesson in how not to drink with coworkers while traveling. Let me first start by saying that there's nothing wrong with having a few drinks with colleagues. But there is a middle ground between casual drinking and making a fool of yourself in public. Even though you are traveling with a coworker, it's always best to keep your guard up. Even if you are on your way home from celebrating a big win for the company, you should still maintain a certain level of professionalism.

Don't be a stick-in-the-mud—no one likes a square—just know your limit and stick to it. I prefer to treat all interactions with coworkers as still being on the clock. Think of it this way: how many drinks would you have if your boss was there? That's how many you should have with colleagues. No more. Don't think for a minute that tales of any rowdy or inappropriate behavior won't get back to your boss. They will—and fast. Consider the situation above. What if it were you who got drunk and belligerent in front of your colleagues? It could be a career ender for sure.

MODERN MANNERS GUY QUIZ

You are on a plane traveling for work with your boss. You want to make a good impression while you have the opportunity, but are nervous about kicking up a conversation. What do you do?

A Flip open the laptop and start pounding away at a very important document to make it clear that you're a dedicated employee who can't go five minutes without working.

B Ignore him. He must be too busy to want to bother talking to you.

C Focus solely on making his flight the best it can possibly be by ensuring that the flight attendants get his drink order right, that he has enough light to read, that he has both armrests, and of course, by carrying his bags (on top of your own) through the airport.

D Make polite conversation about family, recent news, movies, or a hobby like local sports that you know your boss is into. Purposely choose topics other than your last quarter earnings.

Answer

D As shocking as it may sound, your boss is a human being with varied interests and does not always want to talk about work. Not to mention the fact that if you are on a trip with your boss, you are probably already at a level where you don't have to present a Power Point of your achievements at all times. Also, your boss is a big boy or girl—they don't need a servant to make sure their every need is catered to during the flight. They can carry their own bags, pour their own drink, and yes, even fluff their own bacteria-infested in-flight pillow.

Traveling with your boss is nerve-racking and that's understandable. And they understand that. Every CEO I spoke with told me that they know how uneasy people get when traveling with a superior. We often feel like we're on a traveling interview of sorts. So instead of ignoring him (bad idea), or becoming his slave (even worse), use the time to talk about an idea or project that you've wanted to discuss.

Bring it up casually and if you encounter any resistance, drop it. Don't push it and certainly don't dwell on it. And if you find your boss is going for their book or headphones, take that as your signal to do the same. Read a book, listen to music, or take a nap (just don't snore, drool, or slump over their seat).

MODERN MANNERS GUY'S BUSINESS TRAVEL ETIQUETTE TOOL KIT

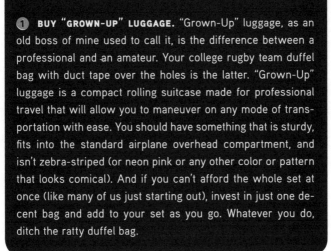

1 **BUY "GROWN-UP" LUGGAGE.** "Grown-Up" luggage, as an old boss of mine used to call it, is the difference between a professional and an amateur. Your college rugby team duffel bag with duct tape over the holes is the latter. "Grown-Up" luggage is a compact rolling suitcase made for professional travel that will allow you to maneuver on any mode of transportation with ease. You should have something that is sturdy, fits into the standard airplane overhead compartment, and isn't zebra-striped (or neon pink or any other color or pattern that looks comical). And if you can't afford the whole set at once (like many of us just starting out), invest in just one decent bag and add to your set as you go. Whatever you do, ditch the ratty duffel bag.

2 **NEVER RELY ON ELECTRONICS.** We've all been on a plane and heard the crew instruct us to "Please turn off all electronic devices." In fact, I was on a flight once and the flight attendant said, "Look y'all, if it's got an on or off button, put it away!" Sure it's easy to go ten or fifteen minutes without your iPad or smartphone, but there is nothing more depressing than turning it back on once you reach 30,000 feet only to realize that you have 8 percent of battery life left . . . and six more hours to go before you reach your destination. That's why you should always pack a hard copy or magazines or books to keep you occupied (unless you like reading a six-month-old *People* that someone left stuffed in the seat-back pocket).

3 **CARRY YOUR MEDS.** My grandmother used to keep a baggie of aspirin in her purse just in case anyone needed some. It was gross. Have you ever swallowed an aspirin that tasted like a roll of pennies? I have, and I don't recommend it. However, what my grandmother did teach me was that it never hurts to have the medication you may need available on hand. Nowadays, we can't always carry all those bottles of prescriptions or creams onto planes due to FAA regulations, so pack whatever meds you need into a small pouch or even one of those pill boxes and keep it in your carry-on. This way, you won't have to suffer when your allergies act up on the dust-filled plane. Or if a colleague (or boss) has one too many gin and tonics on the flight, you can be a hero and offer an aspirin for their headache.

EIGHT

Workplace Relationships

Love is in the air . . . and in the copy room, in the cafeteria, in the gym. Do you know what you're getting yourself into?

Men always want to be a woman's first love—
women like to be a man's last romance.
—Oscar Wilde, writer, poet, instigator

ast month, my friend Pete called to tell me the good news: He had landed the job of his dreams! A week later, after attending a happy hour with his new coworkers, he called me in a panic. "Yeah, so this dream job of mine has truly become a slice of heaven!" I couldn't help but laugh at his sarcasm. Of course I know that a certain amount of disappointment follows starting a new job. Things aren't always as rosy as they seem at first.

Imagine my surprise when I realized that he wasn't being sarcastic. Turns out that nearly every single person he works with, from twenty-five to fifty-five, was attractive. He then went on to list the names of at least seven girls on whom he had developed office crushes. I was happy that my friend's dream job could possibly lead to meeting "the one" but I warned him to tread carefully and keep his crush list private for now.

I didn't want to rain on his parade, but office relationships are not the same thing as relationships that can develop after meeting someone at a bar or being set up by friends. In the workplace, the rules of dating are totally different. In fact, forget *everything* you know about dating in general. The office is not a playground for your hormones or a frat party where everyone is gathered in one area just to hook up. At work, dating is a far second to the real goal of being there. Dare I say it . . . work?

Don't misunderstand. I'm not a downer on love. In fact, I'm a huge romantic and my motto is not only that love is in the air, but that it can easily hit you when you least expect it. The issue here is that an office relationship is a serious matter that can affect not only your social life, but also your job, your livelihood, and your professional reputation. The good news is that you can have a successful relationship (or more than one) while being a productive employee. It's all about timing.

Wanting to date someone you work with is bound to happen. If a new attractive person joins the team, everyone will be thinking the same thing: "Are they single?" And if you are single too and begin to develop feelings, you will most likely start to wonder how you'd go about asking out the new office hottie. However, this takes a lot more than simply putting on your nicest outfit, smelling delicious, and having a killer opener (please, don't act like you don't have an opener).

The Pros Weigh In: LISA LOEB
Grammy-nominated singer/songwriter

• • •

Whenever I think of someone who can best explain how the heart operates, I don't look to medicine, I look to art. Art—whether good or bad, visual or audio—starts and ends with passion. And what better place to look for that passion than my first love? The year was 1994 and the song "Stay (I Missed You)" was number one in the U.S. My fragile teenage heart melted at the sight of her: the cat-eye-glasses-wearing singer with the purring voice. The one and only Lisa Loeb.

Lisa has made a career of crafting beautiful pop ballads (admit it, the chorus to "Stay" is stuck in your head right now), so if there's one person who understands matters of the heart, it's her. And when she kindly let me pick her brain about romance in the workplace, she didn't disappoint. (Nor did she run when I mentioned my youthful crush.)

Unless you arrive at a new job already in a relationship, dating in the workplace is inevitable. If you are going to jump into those dangerous waters, you better be prepared to tread pretty hard because the waves will get bumpy. Mapping out your career is mind-boggling as it is, so when you marry work and romance together (no pun intended), things are unlikely to go swimmingly. Although it *can* happen. I know a few couples who met at work, got married, had kids, and still work in the same company. But just so you know, this scenario is only slightly less rare than a unicorn sighting.

The key to a successful office romance is for both adults to be on the same page. Lisa tells us that in her experience, it's best to be clear with your feelings and goals from the start.

I've dated people I work with—it's just where you end up meeting people. My recommendation is to make sure that all of your legal and contractual business is in order before you jump in. It's important to be clear on your roles and your credit and responsibilities before you get into a project so that if things don't go as expected, you don't have a conflict about it later on. That goes for any working relationship you have, whether it involves dating or not. You can always say, "I know it's a little strange to figure this out in advance, since we don't know where this is going, but I prefer to have our working relationship clear before we start." You might still break up and things might still get messy, but at least being sure that you're on the same page in the beginning makes it a bit easier in the end.

See? Isn't she just perfect? Sigh . . .

Workplace romances have no set rules and they surely have no set outcomes, but as Lisa points out, the best approach is to make sure you both understand the consequences before you jump in headfirst. There is no reason why two people can't—or shouldn't—fall in love at work, they just have to be prepared for what can happen.

Modern Manners Guy's Top 10 Tips on Workplace Relationships

Tip #1: Is It Worth It?

Asking someone out in the office, like deciding to wear your "Charlie Sheen for President" T-shirt in public, comes down to one question: Is it worth it?

Understand that asking out a colleague—even if you don't work together closely—will have a huge impact on your professional career. I'm not trying to say that you will be fired or sequestered to a basement dungeon, but many companies have strict rules on interoffice dating. With that, you have to weigh the pros and cons that come with following your heart (I hope that's what you are following!). Weighing out what can happen (rejection, acceptance, office gossip, disagreements, etc.) versus the potential upside is incredibly important. So before you muster up the courage, step back and take a good look at what you're getting yourself into. Ask yourself, "Is it worth it?" and "Can I handle what could happen?"

If what you're looking for is just a random hookup, then I suggest you fish someplace other than your office pool. The phrase "Don't shit where you eat" comes to mind. Do you really want to put yourself in the position of being bad-mouthed by a spurned ex who happens to have the boss' ear? Not wise.

How to know if the person is worth the risk? Test the waters before jumping in. Become better acquainted to see if you're actually compatible before you suggest a romantic outing. Table the romance for a bit and really find out if you actually have things in common. Mention a book you recently read, a film you saw, a band you like, and then see if their responses line up with yours. If they hate all the things you love, then perhaps it's not worth it. But if this person is someone whom you genuinely like and who seems to return the favor, then perhaps it's worth it to take the plunge and see what happens. The more time you spend with them, the better you can figure out if you want to take it a step further. In the end, I hope your heart gives you the answer you're looking for.

Tip #2: The Friend Zone

We've all been in this situation: You're friends with someone and they're awesome. You have a great time together, you like the same things, you share a sense of humor. Everything's peachy . . . except that you're dying to make things romantic but the other person has no clue. You're trapped in the Friend Zone.

Ah, the Friend Zone—that agonizing relationship in which every time the object of your affection calls you a "friend" it feels like a slap in the face. Yeah, *that* feeling. In fact, most of us would probably take that punch over being called a friend over and over again by the person of our dreams, while they go on and on about someone else they're interested in.

If you've never been in the Friend Zone, here is a sample of how some conversations go: "It's so nice to have a *friend* like you who I can talk to about [insert name here]. I mean, only if *they* were more like *you,* and were such a good *friend,* it would be the perfect relationship!" In case you weren't counting, that's two direct friend references.

Just in case there's any confusion, the Friend Zone does not discriminate. It is a quiet little town where both men and women visit in equal measure. In the workplace, where you get closer to people much faster than in the outside world since you're around each other constantly, you may find yourself passing through the Friend Zone pretty often.

Despite the immediate and daily closeness to a co-worker for whom you've developed feelings, you can't let it affect your job. This isn't middle school where you spend all day jaw dropped, staring at the person of your dreams. Doing *that* will get your fired. Being in the Friend Zone is not the worst thing in the world so don't let it cloud your judgment and productivity. If you want to cross that line, that's fine and I always encourage you to follow your heart (just check out Tip #1 to really figure out if it's worth it). However, in the end, office romances are tougher than normal ones and sometimes being just a "friend" is actually a blessing in disguise.

Granted, settling for friendship is not ideal, but building close friendships with people at work is never a bad consolation prize. Don't write someone off just because they don't see you as "The One." However, if you're really dead set on leaving the Friend Zone and entering Romance City, then don't stick around to listen to how the love of your life and their new partner enjoy acting out scenes from the newest edition of the *Kama Sutra*. If it annoys or upsets you to hear about this person's love life without you in it, then I recommend you pack your bags and leave the Friend Zone at once.

Tip #3: Dating Your Coworker

As I discussed in Tip #2, if you enjoy—or can handle—the sweet and succulent pain of rejection that comes with being just a "friend," well, good for you. Don't get me wrong, having friends is part of what makes life wonderful. However, you are in the minority. Most of us just can't handle seeing yet another photo of our crush's new guy/girl on our Facebook feed. So let's say you've decided to cross the line from friendship to romance, you've weighed the pros and cons of taking that risk, and you've come to a decision. Now, it's time to act.

First things first: Asking a coworker for a date should not happen at work. For one thing, the office gossip factor will always make the start or progress of a relationship more stressful (see chapter 3). Also, no cubicle or office is so private that others won't catch on to what's happening. "Why was Mitch spending so much time by Liz's cube? . . . You know, they've been awfully close lately . . ." Trust me, this type of rumor-mongering occurs pretty often, even if you aren't dating at all!

Secondly, and most important, dating in the office is not something that comes with the paycheck; it's a perk. Your boss does not have to allow it if they don't want to. In fact, many companies have strict rules prohibiting workplace dating entirely. So if you want to ask someone out, do so outside the office—either at lunch with just the two of you or at a separate event. Maybe it takes some more finesse to get the person alone, but it's essential. And when you do ask, be mature enough to keep this between the both of you. No one else has to know until you're ready to go public.

If all goes well and you start dating, it's proper to let your boss know. True, your boss doesn't have the right to tell you how to live your life, but this is their turf. A romantic relationship will inevitably affect the dynamic of the workplace, which means they have a right to know about it. The boss will appreciate your openness and maturity in revealing the situation and doing so will most likely not raise any red flags (unless you work at a stuffy place where any colleague coupling is forbidden). But one key thing to remember when dating someone at work is that *productivity trumps romance*. If you had a fight the night before and can't work together the next day because of it, that's a problem. If by dating someone you spend more time in their office than at your desk, that's a problem as well. If you use your position with your partner as leverage to improve your status in the company, that is an improper use of your relationship, and it will likely come back to bite you.

Tip #4: PDA in the Office

Whether it's true love or a short-lived affair, when you're dating someone you want to show them how you feel at every opportunity. When it's in the office, you'll get coffee together, have lunch, and generally spend more time than normal in each other's space. Makes sense, right? So you head down to the cafeteria, grab a table for two, or flirt around the coffeemaker in the kitchen. However, that's where it should end. The company cafeteria is not a romantic getaway where you get to cuddle up together in a booth. There is a time and place for public displays of affection (PDAs) and lunchtime on company property is neither the time nor the place.

If you're in the middle of Central Park having a picnic and love is in the air, there's no reason you and your special someone can't "enjoy" your time together (clothes on though, folks). Or if you're dining at a nice restaurant and want to pull your sweetie close to you like a cheesy jewelry commercial, then go for it. However, when you are at work the level of PDA should be toned down drastically. And when I say "toned down," I mean just don't do it. This isn't high school where people feverishly rush to make out in dark corners during the break between classes as if they'll never see one another again. When you dine in the office cafeteria, make your professional side shine brighter than your burning passion. The same goes for groping in the kitchen. It's just tacky. Save it for after hours.

Tip #5: Dating Your Boss

By far, the most complicated interoffice dating situation is when you're dating someone you work for—or someone who works for you. This is the ultimate recipe for disaster. Even if the boss is the most respected, forward-thinking person in the world, and the employee in the relationship is the smartest and most professional, there will always be an ethical gray area when you mix business with pleasure (sorry, couldn't help myself). No matter how well you carry yourself in the workplace, all the other employees will automatically assume that there's favoritism and this assumption will color your every interaction with colleagues.

A Modern Manners Guy fan named Rob e-mailed me about a sticky situation. He was dating his female boss. They hit it off from day one and despite a five-year age gap (which is not a lot), found that they had similar tastes. So, long story short, he approached her tentatively, asked her out for a drink after work, and they began dating. They kept it quiet for four months until they finally came out to the rest of the office. They didn't announce their love via skywriting or in a mass e-mail, but they simply stopped sneaking around and if anyone asked, they would happily admit to the relationship. She cleared it with the other top executives, which was the proper thing to do. Kudos to both Rob and his boss for having the courage to be up-front!

Although Rob's colleagues were happy for him, it quickly became clear that they viewed him differently. People got quiet when he walked into the kitchen, or if they passed him in the hallway. When there was word of a promotion in the office, everyone assumed that he was instantly the top candidate. He felt as though everyone was judging his—and the boss'—professionalism based on their relationship.

Now, as sad as his coworkers were, their reaction is unavoidable. It's the same thing as working with the boss' family member; no matter what they do—good or bad— everyone knows that the emotional attachment to loved ones has the potential to cloud judgment. I mean, let's say you worked at Rob's company and suddenly extreme budget cuts were announced. If you were fired while Rob's job was safe, you couldn't help but think there was favoritism afoot.

If you are dating your boss, the proper thing to do is to remove yourself from their immediate report. Wait, wait,

wait, I'm not saying you have to quit! But if you are *dating*—not married, not engaged to—someone who signs your paycheck or is in control of your career, emotions will always get in the way. That's why it's essential to act maturely and try to maintain a clear head. So try to alter your position to work for someone else. Chances are, your boss will be able to pull some strings.

Tip #6: The Unofficial Relationship

One of the questions I am asked most often is about relationships that are not quite "official" yet. You know what I'm talking about: the time period following a few dates or hookups when you log onto Facebook every day, wondering if your special someone had changed their status from "Single" to "In a Relationship" yet. Until they publicly announce this monumental shift in their status to their closest 2,000 "friends," or heaven forbid you both actually talk about it, you're stuck in that awkward purgatory known as the "unofficial relationship." And to make matters worse, if this is happening with a colleague, you have to see them every day at work and be reminded of the unspoken question. So you walk on eggshells around them, not wanting to be too clingy, but then again, not wanting to seem uninterested. It's exhausting.

If you really think about it, the time you've spent with someone you're dating at work by far surpasses any other non-workplace relationship of the same length. I mean, when you're dating someone you met outside of work, you only see them at night and on the weekends. If it works out, you may meet up for lunch, but that's rarely the case. So a relationship in the office tends to run at an expedited rate, just because you see the person more frequently. For this reason, it makes jumping from "Where are we?" to "You're the one!" seem somewhat rushed.

But it shouldn't.

In any relationship, the issue of "time" is always looming over you:

- How often should we see each other?
- When is the right time to introduce them to my friends?
- When can I post pictures of us together on Facebook?
- How long before we have "The Talk"?

If you date someone outside of the office, it will take longer to feel them out and really learn if you're compatible. But if you spend the majority of your day with someone, there's a faster learning curve. You'll be able to see them in a rainbow of emotions and situations (stressed, happy, mad, nervous, quiet, talkative, etc.). This may actually be a saving grace because it'll allow you to form a quicker opinion on whether this will work out or not.

Nonetheless, it still doesn't mean you should rush to go from unofficial to official. But if you do see them in an unflattering light, this is a good time to go from "unofficial" to "next!" Timing is key in relationships and there is nothing wrong with being unofficial until you are both ready to change status.

Tip #7: The Random Office Hookup

Man, oh man, was that holiday party awesome! The venue, the music, the drinks . . . oh yeah, the drinks. Nah, you didn't have that much . . . or did you? And damn it, wouldn't you know, your roommate apparently snuck into your bed and is now sleeping next to you. Wait . . . wait a second! Oh, that's right, it's your coworker from the marketing department. Remember?

As we talked about earlier in this chapter, being attracted to someone you work with is natural and wanting to ask them out is going to cross your mind. But what happens when you skip the "asking them out" step and jump right into "making out"? This is what I like to call the "Random Office Hookup" and it rarely ends well.

Like the unofficial relationship, there is a level of awkwardness that occurs in both scenarios. However, in the unofficial relationship, you don't regret going to lunch with someone because you clearly made plans and are both on board. The random office hookup though, well, therein lies the problem. The random office hookup is not as thought out and planned as other dating situations in the office. In fact, it's not planned at all!

You were both having a little too much fun, one thing led to another, and now you have something totally different to talk about at the water cooler than the weather. But talking about what happened is the proper way to handle things. This conversation does not have to be lengthy either. Don't feel like you need to go to couples counseling! Simply step away from the spying eyes at the office and discuss what happened. This can go in one of two ways:

1. If you thought it was a mistake, say, "Look, about last night . . . I'm not quite ready for a relationship. I'm sorry if I led you on. I didn't intend to and I apologize."
2. If you want to take things further, say, "Look, about last night . . . I'm actually glad it happened and I hope to see you again. But let's start with a coffee after work next Thursday. Does that work for you?"

And of course you'll both say that this type of thing "never happens to me."

Right. Sure.

However you handle the random office hookup, whether you view it as a mistake or a miracle, you have to talk about it with your coworker. Dating in the office is serious for your career and you don't want someone to view you as a "snake" or even a "coward" for running from the situation. Grow a pair, step up, rip off the Band-Aid, and other clichés.

Tip #8: How to Handle Being Stood Up

Modern Manners Guy fans who have e-mailed me about being stood up all voiced similar feelings: "It's so embarrassing!" . . . "I felt betrayed" . . . "We were just finalizing plans that day and then they don't show up!" And if the person who stood you up is a work colleague, someone you have to face every day, it burns twice as much.

If this has happened to you (and if it hasn't yet, it likely will in the future), take a page from the Steve McQueen playbook. The film legend was known as the "King of Cool," which is pretty much the most badass nickname in Hollywood history. Although no one can pull off the calm swagger of the King himself, there's a lot to be said about being able to keep your ego and temper in check when faced with an embarrassing situation like being stood up.

I know you probably spent all day thinking about your date, from the clothes you'll wear to the conversation you'll have. But then you find yourself waiting at the restaurant or bar for ten minutes too long . . . then fifteen . . . then twenty . . . then thirty! You check your phone and get nothing. You check your e-mail—nothing. This is the digital age, when smartphones rule all, so there is no excuse why someone can't get in touch with you (unless they're stuck underground).

Then slowly, as much as you wished it wasn't so, it dawns on you that you've been stood up. Do you stay at the bar, get wasted, and rant the no-show's name to anyone who will listen? No way! In times like this, remember McQueen and play it cool. Do you think Steve ever got all bent of shape when he was stood up? Hell no! Okay, so maybe that didn't happen to him very often, considering that he was one of Hollywood's most epic sex symbols. But my point still stands. You don't have to be a gorgeous celebrity to keep your cool.

First off, realize you're not the first to be stood up, you're not the last, and sadly it may happen again in one way or another in your life. Did you waste your time? Yes. Does it suck that the person didn't have the basic manners to call and cancel? Absolutely!

However, that is where the emotional roller coaster should end. If you allow yourself to dwell on the situation, it will only make you more upset or bitter. I recommend staying at that bar/restaurant, but instead of drowning your sorrows in several rounds of Maker's Mark, call up one of your friends to meet you. Heck, call two or three. Don't waste the outfit and make it a night out. Order the nicest dish on the menu and enjoy the good company. And if that deadbeat ever does call back to apologize, tell them it's okay—you had a great time without them! And no, you don't want to reschedule, thank you very much.

If you'd still like to give the person a chance (it's possible that some unforeseen circumstance, like a death in the family or a cat drowning, actually prevented them from getting in touch), you can save face by leaving them the following message: "Hey [name of rude person], I thought we were supposed to meet at the restaurant at 7:30. I'm guessing you got held up. Don't worry, it's cool. I hope everything is okay. Just call me another time and we can reschedule. Have a good night."

What you're doing here is giving them a chance to explain themselves when they call you back. If they don't, then you've behaved like the bigger person and know that they don't deserve your time. Win-win!

The business world has a cruel corollary to being stood up. It's called The Corporate Ditch, and it happens when you've tried for a while to get a meeting with someone for business reasons and, after finally nailing down a meeting time, you are stood up. Granted, this is not a romantic event, but being stood up for a business meeting still burns. You've done your research, you've prepared your pitch, and you've waited all week to finally, *finally,* have this meeting . . . only to be greeted with a voice mail. So what do you do?

Don't rant. Don't send an angry e-mail that you'll regret. And definitely don't burn bridges. Instead, leave a casual voice mail message to let them know you understand they may have gotten busy, explain how much you looked forward to the meeting, and set another time to meet. Try something like, "Hi [name of rude jerk] I guess you got held up this afternoon. Not a problem. I'm going to head out because I have another meeting across town, but let's plan on getting together next Tuesday, same time and place. Does that work? Let me know. Thanks again."

This tactic forces a response. So whether they call back

and accept the new meeting time or refuse, at least you'll know exactly where you stand and won't waste any more of your valuable time.

Tip #9: How to Handle a Workplace Breakup

I've said it before and I'll say it again: One of the most important rules in business is "don't burn bridges." That means it's always best to maintain civil, polite relations with people after ending a relationship (of any kind). This is even more true for ending a workplace romance. The last thing you want is to be known as some heartless creature who callously breaks up with their girl/boyfriend via text.

A friend of mine recently told me that he was ending a relationship. When I asked how, he said, matter-of-factly, "It depends. Text. E-mail is always good. Or just stop calling. She'll get the idea." As you can imagine, his now ex-girlfriend did not quite "get the idea." After hearing my friend's pathetic, cowardly means to an end, I was shocked. What happened to us? Is this the new norm? Have all the John Cusack and Julia Roberts movies led me down a path of naïveté?

Option #1: Text

Before we get to that question, let's establish something about texting: It's the lowest and laziest form of communication. Alexander Graham Bell invented the telephone because typing letters wasn't efficient enough. Now, over one hundred years later—when we have cell phones and Internet in the palms of our hands—people find it necessary to revert back to the 1800s and type a message. Do you see the irony?

The texting breakup has become stuff of pop culture legend, made famous a few years back when Taylor Swift claimed that her Jonas Brother love ended their romance via text. What was this guy thinking? I'm not just talking about the fact that this girl has a face sent from heaven, but Jo-Bro, this girl will make you (even more) famous if you mess with her heart! And not in a good way. This is not news. But I digress.

If you are going to ruin someone's happiness for the day (or weekend . . . or month), texting is not the way to do it. A text breakup casts a nasty shadow on the entire relationship, as if to say it was never that important anyway. No matter how eloquent you try to make a text breakup, this is how it reads: "Hey, there, I'm about to walk into the office but wanted to tell you it's just not working for me. Best of luck. Hope we can still be friends?" Yeah right, *friends*? Are you kidding me?

If you've just been dumped by text, delete it immediately and try to move on—even if moving on means a carton of Ben & Jerry's. This type of cowardice does not deserve a response.

Option #2: E-mail

A breakup text's slightly nicer, but still tacky, cousin is the breakup e-mail. You can write pages of reasons why you are ending the relationship, but it won't help—you're still a wimp if you don't have the cojones to look the person in the eye. The only upside to the e-mail breakup is that it's a step up from the text breakup, which is like saying a kick in the head is a step up from a kick in the crotch.

Yes, people tend to be more open and honest through e-mail than in person, but that doesn't make ending things through e-mail any better. My friend Erica told me she prefers to do it this way because it "Hurts her less." Hurts *her* less? What about the poor sap whose heart you just destroyed? The dumpee always gets hurt more, no matter how guilty the dumper may feel. If you're the e-mail dumpee, don't reply right away. First of all, you are pissed—which you should be—and second, it will drive them crazy waiting to hear what you have to say. Bonus!

Option #3: Phone

As I said earlier, the telephone was invented to make communication easier and faster, but that does not mean it should be in your breakup arsenal. This is the pound-for-pound world champion of rude relationship behavior. I mean, how old are we?

You should never end a relationship by not calling. It's a colossal step back in our evolution. Instead of falling off the planet, try instead to—drum roll—just be honest! Oh yes, honesty and consideration, the little things that separate us from beasts in the wild. By being honest you'll save yourself tons of frustration. Chances are you'll run into this person again (especially if you work together) and the last thing you need is for them to remember you as the one who never called, e-mailed, or—and I can't believe I'm saying this—texted back.

Option #4: In Person

It may be hard, but the only truly proper way to break up with someone you're dating at work is in person. You have to make things clear, concise, and final. Simply tell them that you just don't feel the way you did before. Tell them it's best to end things now before it goes on and they end up hating you. Never say, "We can still be friends." It's lame and weak and if you are meant to be friends, it will turn out that way—but it'll be the dumpee's job to decide if they're interested in your friendship.

If you're dating someone at work and you don't want to be involved anymore, tell them you are not ready for a full-on commitment. Yes, you thought you were when you started the relationship, but realized you need to figure things out for yourself and don't want to make things weird between you two because you work together. Whether it lasted a week, a month, or even a year, let them know you tried but just weren't ready. They won't like that answer and may feel like you were leading them on, but it certainly beats simply disappearing. Because nothing says revenge like a spurned lover going to HR and saying the two magic words that can derail your career forever: sexual harassment. (What did you think I was going to say?)

"Really, Kenny, really?!? An e-mail breakup?
I'm sitting right here!"

Being up-front is not always the easiest way, but in the end it's the honorable thing to do. I guarantee you, if you cared for them at all, they will appreciate it (eventually). Just note, they may throw a drink in your face, so duck and cover.

Tip #10: The Serial Office Dater

As we've seen, dating in the workplace has its pros and cons, which you must take into consideration whenever you decide to jump into a relationship. You must also take into consideration how many times you jump. Sadly, if you are known as the serial office dater, it may hinder your chances of finally meeting the person you are truly meant to date because they'll think you'll burn right through them like you did with the rest. Yes, people talk. No, nothing is sacred. Don't expect anything to stay hidden for long in the workplace.

The serial dater takes two forms:

1. Someone who doesn't intend to become a serial dater, but when you spend forty to sixty hours a week in one setting, you are bound to run into people you are interested in. It's only natural and perfectly understandable.
2. Someone who treats their dating life as a game, with the end goal of adding as many notches to their record as possible.

For one, there is no harm in dating multiple people in your office—not at the same time, of course! But given how much time you spend with your colleagues versus with strangers in bars, it's bound to happen. For example, my coworker Andrew told me that he was worried about his reputation because he's dated six colleagues in five years. He is a clean-cut, well-respected, attractive, fun guy, so dating has always been fairly easy for him. But finding the right one was not. And that's what he was looking for.

Is that his fault? Should he be labeled a serial dater simply because he wants to fall in love? No, he should not. And the only way to safely date at work and keep your reputation from going south is by following the tips I mentioned earlier in this chapter:

1. Weigh the pros and cons of dating a particular person.
2. Minimize the office gossip that comes about as the result of your relationship (aka, provide them as little information as possible to stir rumors).
3. Don't break up badly. This could be the ultimate reputation (and career) ruiner.
4. Never intentionally lead someone on.

Bottom line is that an office relationship must be handled more delicately than any other one, so treating everyone with respect and kindness is the only way to pull off dating multiple people in the office.

However, if your only goal is to be able to say, "Yeah, I did that," well, guess what—you're a pig. Oh, and I hope you get fired, too. Man or woman, anyone who thinks that dating is only for bragging rights has clearly never evolved past age sixteen. Even at that age it's foul, but as an adult? Come on, grow up. If you want to go on a rampage of sexual escapades, go right ahead. But if you think you can pull this off in the office, you are wrong. Not only will you look bad in your peers' eyes, you could also easily be fired for creating an unprofessional working environment. Plus, when you really do fall for someone, they'll want nothing to do with you, given your "player" reputation.

MODERN MANNERS GUY QUIZ

After two months of dating someone in your office, you realize it's just not working out. So one night after work you e-mail them and end it as politely as you can. The next day, they are still e-mailing you at work asking "Why? Why? Whyyyyyyy?" You can't get anything done and are afraid to even see them. How do you deal with this situation?

A Take the person back after e-mail #52. After all, they did just score front-row tickets to the concert you've been dying to go to. What's another couple of weeks?

B After realizing this person is a Level 1 whack-job, tell your boss and HR about what happened. Present the e-mail thread as proof and let them know that this situation is now affecting your job performance.

C Walk over to their desk and "rip them a new one" in front of everyone to make sure they firmly understand where you stand on not wanting to pursue the relationship.

D Ignore them completely, hoping they'll just get the hint.

Answer

B . . . with a hint of D. Allow me to explain.

Let's face it, we're all much quicker to jump into bed with someone than we are to do a background check to see how (in)sane they are. And as many of us know all too well, sometimes the craziest ones are the best looking, which tends to dim the freak-o-meter until we realize they've caught us in their web of weirdness. Happens all the time. So don't feel bad that you didn't see this coming. However, just because they can't handle the breakup doesn't mean you should accept angry e-mails, rants, or any other borderline crazy antics. Immediately tell your boss and HR that this is becoming an issue. If they e-mail you asking why you don't love them anymore, that's understandable. But if it's name-calling or threats, don't wait to take it to your manager. Even if you don't want HR to "take action" yet, at least let them know it's starting to affect your work. That's something they will definitely care about.

In terms of sprinkling a little D into your approach, what I mean is that you don't freeze them out completely, but you don't want to bait them into a bigger argument by constantly feeding their e-mail thread. Don't get sucked into a discussion, over e-mail or in person. Let them e-mail you until their fingers hurt, but don't retaliate and turn this little fire into a barn burner. Chances are, this can lead you down a road with no end and also make you say something out of anger that you may regret.

MODERN MANNERS GUY'S WORKPLACE RELATIONSHIPS TOOL KIT

1 THE OFFICE PRENUP. No, I don't mean an actual written document but an informal agreement. Like Lisa Loeb said, it's always good to know where you stand before the relationship so if it does end, everyone leaves with what they brought to the table. This means if you are working closely with someone you're dating, make sure that you both understand your contributions so there's no finger-pointing later on. Being partners at work and partners in love is not the same thing.

2 BREAKUP DOCUMENTS. Breakups always become a case of "he said, she said." That's why you should always save the e-mails from your office romance, especially ones where the "true self" of your (in)significant other comes out. This way, when they say, "I never said that!" you can show them that "Well, yeah, you kinda did."

3 KEEP YOUR OWN SPACE. I once had a colleague who let his girlfriend use his big corner office as a "hideout" to unwind or have lunch in during the day. Since they were dating, he didn't mind her popping in while he was on a call or working. However, she made herself more comfortable by inviting friends, as if it was her office, too. When the relationship ended, she still felt entitled to use his office as she did before. Sadly, this is not how it works. Here's a perfect example of why the Office Prenup from Tip #1 is a good idea.

4 IXNAY THE PDA. When you're in love, you want to shout it from the rooftops. However, there is a time and a place for that and work is not it. So save the PDA for after hours and weekends. You might actually find it exciting to "abstain" during the day—and rip each other's clothes off at night. You know what they say: absence makes the heart grow fonder.

NINE

The Unwritten Rules of Career Success

The ass you kick on the way up is the ass you kiss on the way down—and many other unwritten rules from top industry professionals.

This chapter is by far my favorite since it cuts down to the bare-bones honest truth about what really separates success from failure in the business world. It's one thing to know how to dress for a job interview, or how to handle an obnoxious coworker (both of which are key), but it's quite another to have unique insights directly from the pros about what you should and shouldn't do to advance your career.

Each of my interviews with the experts you find throughout this book ended with a question about the unwritten rules of success. And every time I brought up this idea of unwritten rules, I could almost see them roll up their sleeves over the phone (or through e-mail). Although they are leaders in a wide variety of industries, you'll notice quite a few common threads in their responses.

And that's no accident. The basic tenets of decorum and respect are universal and can apply to almost any occupation.

Modern Manners Guy's Top 25 Unwritten Rules of Manners and Etiquette in the Business World

#1: Be Humble

Jonathan Monaghan, world-renowned artist and animator

Being inexperienced and at the same time arrogant is not going to get you too far. You have to be willing to learn and put in the hard work. That's how you can improve your knowledge and skills and learn to work well with others, which are key for success.

#2: Preparation Is Everything

Lyndon and Jamie Cormack, founders of Herschel Supply Co.

Don't feel as though you have to know everything right away. Part of being new is being able to admit that you don't know something, but that you are committed to research the answer.

#3: Learn What You Don't Know

Steve Guttenberg, actor and author

My best advice to someone just starting out in the entertainment industry is read, read, read. Know the classics. Know nineteenth- and twentieth-century works. Read fiction and non-fiction, see plays, see the AFI 100 movies, see opera and ballet, go to museums, go to bookstores.

#4: Keep It Simple

Steve Abrams, CEO of Magnolia Bakery

I don't like when people waste my time. I'm a very quick study. I like things to be as simple and direct as possible. Don't overcomplicate things. You will lose me, and my interest in doing business with you ... Keep it simple.

#5: Thank You Never Gets Old

Andrew Buerger, cofounder of B'more Organic

Always say "Thank you." My two-year-old twins say it all the time and so should adults. Whether it's a leader thanking subordinates, a service provider thanking customers, or—what no one seems to do—customers thanking vendors (after all, most work very hard on your behalf), a little thanks goes a long way.

#6: Make Yourself Available

Spike Mendelsohn, restaurateur and Top Chef

I'm a pretty tolerant guy, but I get frustrated when people don't make themselves available in the professional world. A lot of projects that I work on involve coordinating phone calls between people on opposite coasts, all of whom have crazy schedules. You have to be flexible and understand that work doesn't just happen from 9 to 5. Sometimes you have a call at 11 p.m. because that is when it needs to happen.

#7: Value People

Jolanta Benal, author of *The Dog Trainer's Complete Guide to a Happy, Well-Behaved Pet*

It's a bad idea to price-shop professionals. The cheapest one in your market is rarely the best qualified.

#8: Body Language Speaks Volumes

Neil Blumenthal, cofounder of Warby Parker

Some of the basics are often overlooked: sit up straight, look people in the eye, and practice a firm handshake. Body language is crucial to being a professional. [When we're hiring], we're not just looking for a person who can handle the job, we're also looking for someone to grow in the company. If they don't have manners, a physical presence, or leadership potential, then we really don't want to waste the time bringing them in and training them.

"As you can see, I graduated top of my class, with a 4.0, so I'm qualified for anything you have . . . just as long as I don't have to talk to people . . . or work in groups . . . or go to parties . . ."

#9: Be Aware of Personal Space

Mignon Fogarty, bestselling author of *Grammar Girl's Quick and Dirty Tips for Better Writing*
I wish people would resist reclining their seats on airplanes. Yes, you're allowed to recline, but doing so makes the person behind you uncomfortable

(well, more uncomfortable) for the entire flight, and it often makes it nearly impossible to use a laptop. When people are confined together in such a small space, they should strive to be extra considerate of one another.

#10: Look the Part

Louis Black, cofounder of SXSW and of *The Austin Chronicle*

Dress well, be soft spoken, and show good manners. No matter how brilliant you are or how great your work is, a lot of [your success or failure] comes from how you come across to others.

#11: Not All Billionaires Wear Suits

Steven Robbins, Harvard MBA and author of *Get-It-Done Guy's 9 Steps to Work Less and Do More*

People often make assumptions about who is and isn't important based on age, bearing, and attire. This is not only rude, it's also dangerous. In today's world, middle-aged con men wear suits and twenty-eight-year-old billionaires wear jeans. Treat everyone with respect and you'll be pleased with the result. As a longtime techie, I've never been comfortable in anything except jeans, and I look much younger than my age. People often pass me by at networking events because of my appearance. That's why I started doing public speaking—it established my credibility.

#12: Know Your Comfort Level

Pranav Vora, founder of Hugh & Crye
Do not get too comfortable with your coworkers. It's great to build friendships at work, but getting too friendly can sometimes lead to losing sight of the fact that there's a professional relationship that matters even more than the personal.

#13: Be Honest, Brutally Honest . . .

Sam Tarantino, cofounder/CEO of Grooveshark
Always be honest even if it means being brutally honest. People respect those who call it like it is. If someone you work for doesn't appreciate total honesty, then you shouldn't work for them because it's a sign of bad leadership.

#14: . . . But Not So Honest That It Comes Back to Bite You

Beata Santora, editor-in-chief of QuickAndDirtyTips.com
Honesty in the workplace is great . . . unless you work for someone who can't take it. If you find

yourself on the receiving end of a cold shoulder because you chose to tell your boss exactly what you thought of their product idea or their management style, then think twice about the honesty route. Sometimes it's better to smile, bite your tongue, and agree than to be totally honest and make your point. Or else you might wind up in charge of coffee runs and copies.

#15: Value Your Connections

Rob Samuels, COO of Maker's Mark

[Success] is not about meeting expectations, it's about exceeding expectations. We go to great lengths to connect with folks in a meaningful way. When we deal with each other in our team, it's all about honesty and transparency.

#16: Don't Run From Confrontation

Brian Duncanson, cofounder and head of strategic planning for the Spartan Race

Deal with personality issues directly whenever possible. Better to meet them head on and break through your differences rather than allowing them to linger.

#17: Always Return Phone Calls

Steve Guttenberg, actor and author

Behaviors that are unacceptable are unreturned phone calls or letters. There is a civil mandate in show business: return a call or letter promptly. The more important the person, the quicker he will return your call. The idiots take their sweet time. The consequences are a bitch. You may need that person later. And try getting your call returned then.

#18: Respond to E-mail Promptly

Benjamin August, screenwriter and producer

In this day and age, it's absolutely beyond rude to not reply to an e-mail in a timely manner. There's few among us who don't check their e-mail every 2.5 seconds whether or not we're in the office. There's nothing worse than going to lunch with someone who spends more than half the meal typing on their BlackBerry or iPhone. However, when you send them a message, it seems as if you're using the U.S. postal system. You don't need to write an essay. You just need to answer relevant questions with firm answers. If you don't have the answer yet, you can say, "I'll get back to you on that." Business is business. It shouldn't feel like dating when you start to wonder, "Why isn't he/she writing me back?"

#19: Don't Exaggerate in E-mail

Lisa B. Marshall, author of *Smart Talk: The Public Speaker's Guide to Success in Every Situation*
Stop using exclamation points in e-mail!!!!

Don't assume that what you think is urgent is necessarily also urgent to the recipient . . . it rarely is. Instead write better subject lines that precisely summarize the point of your e-mail: "Urgent Reply Needed by 5pm re: marketing plan update."

#20: Step Away from the Phone

Lisa Loeb, Grammy-nominated singer/songwriter
It's bad manners to answer e-mails on your smartphone or computer while in a meeting with someone (without excusing yourself first or even acknowledging that you're doing it).

#21: Meet a Person—In Person

Damon Young, author and contributing editor at Ebony.com
With us becoming more and more dependent on the Internet and other forms of communication technology, it helps to remember that dealing

with an actual human—whether face-to-face or just a voice over the phone—matters.

#22: Don't Always Be Selling

Amanda Thomas, owner of Moxie Girl Household Assistants and host of the Domestic CEO podcast

When at a networking event, simply present who you are and what you do. If people want to buy your service or product, they will tell you. If they don't tell you they want it, don't try and sell it to them. Ever! It's a total turnoff.

#23: Hygiene Is Key

Ben Greenfield, fitness expert and author of *Get-Fit Guy's Guide to Achieving Your Ideal Body*

If you have a company gym, I recommend using it often. But if there's no opportunity to shower afterwards, I don't recommend covering up body odor with excessive fragrance. That can potentially annoy or distract your colleagues. Instead, I've found that most exercise odor can be fixed with this quick trick: Smear a bit of coconut oil on your underarms and you'll smell slightly tropical, without overpowering the noses around you. Alternatively, use a stick of basic, no-frills, baking-soda-based antiperspirant—and save the fancy smells for your hot dates, not your business functions.

#24: Bad Breath = Bad for Business

Eugene Foley, president of Foley Entertainment, Inc.
If you've eaten onions, garlic, or anything else that could be offensive before a business meeting, please freshen your breath. Sitting across from that person for an hour is not enjoyable.

#25: Make Magic

Ken Austin, cofounder of Marquis Jet and founder/ CEO of Tequila Avión
Think about how you can create magic in everything you do, so people can look at you and say "There's something there . . . I wish I could do that."

Afterword:
The Etiquette Renaissance

When people hear that I'm Modern Manners Guy, the one question they usually ask is: *Do you think etiquette is dead?*

I don't blame them. If you based the answer to this question on the current lineup of television programming on practically any channel, the answer would be a clear "Yes!"

But why is this? Why have manners taken a back seat lately? Maybe we're too obsessed with our social media relationships to pay attention to the real ones. Maybe it's because some people still foolishly believe that it's cool to act like a jerk. Maybe watching reality shows where people treat each other like garbage has made bad behavior seem normal. It's a toss-up. However, I believe the real reason is that the idea of being "mannerly" or having proper etiquette tends to get confused with being "old-fashioned," which seems lame and uncool.

For some strange reason, manners are often seen as something that you rebelled against as a child. It's as if growing up in a household where you said "Please" and "Thank you" somehow makes you appear uptight or stuck-up. So there is an immediate divide between the stuffy folks who know which fork goes with the foie gras and everyone else, who are more like Will Ferrell's character from *Wedding Crashers* lounging around in their underwear yelling, "Hey Ma! Can we get some meatloaf?"

But that's just not true. Manners aren't just the domain of "old fogies" who believe they are better than everyone else because they know which Cabernet Sauvignon goes with the chateaubriand or how to fold a napkin into a swan. Think you can't display proper etiquette at a backyard barbeque where the Cabernet and steak are replaced with beer and burgers? Sure you can! Acquiring manners is the practice of learning from past mistakes and making sure you don't put your foot in your mouth again . . . while using the wrong fork.

So it's time we stop pretending that having manners is only reserved for older people or characters on *Downton Abbey*. It's time we rethink the idea that you can't balance being mannerly and being cool or current—as if one must necessarily exclude the other. Manners is not something you're born with and it's certainly not something you should be afraid to acquire simply because you think being cool is shouting expletives in public for a cheap laugh.

How is that cool? Funny, maybe, if real life was a movie. But it's not, so drop the act. Manners are readily available to anyone willing to give their mind a much-needed wake-up call.

And that's why my answer to the question "Is etiquette dead?" is a resounding "No!" Far from being dead, manners and etiquette are actually experiencing a renaissance. That's right, manners are back in style like fitted suits and Wayfarers. Don't believe me? Then ask yourself: Why did you decide to pick up this book? Perhaps you're tired of witnessing blatantly unmannerly behavior that makes you roll your eyes, mutter under your breath, and wonder if we're all going to hell in a handbasket. Perhaps you're one of those smart people who realize that manners *matter* a great deal and you want to do everything in your power to hone your behavior and elevate your career.

And if this is what you think, then you're absolutely right!

Every single CEO, entrepreneur, and tastemaker who I interviewed for this book told me that people with good manners are rare to find. So when they come across an employee or colleague who can carry on a lucid conversation without checking their phone every five seconds, or actually says "Thank you" when appropriate, or arrives to a meeting on time and prepared, they take notice. That's why manners and etiquette are now at a level of cool like never before—I'm talking Steve McQueen on a motorcycle, Justin Timberlake on *SNL*, and *Mad Men* kind of cool—because they have a huge impact on our professional success.

So, is etiquette dead?

Not at all!

It may be bruised a bit, but thanks to you, it's more alive than ever.

Acknowledgments

Although this book is my voice, it took a fantastic team to make it sing. First and foremost, I would like to thank my amazing editor Beata Santora, who sacrificed her time and sanity to put up with me during this process. There is not enough aspirin in the world to cure the headaches I caused her over the past year. Her role included persistent management of everything from the smallest details to the big picture, having to use so much red ink that she should have bought stock in Bic and, of course, keeping me motivated when timelines crept up. And kudos to her for doing it all with a smile. She not only fought to make this book happen but used her magic wand to mold it into my dream come true.

Thanks to Emily Rothschild for giving me my first shot at being Modern Manners Guy.

Thanks to the wonderful folks at Macmillan, St. Martin's Press, and QuickAndDirtyTips.com who have given me the opportunity to present Modern Manners Guy to the world. Your support and belief in me is immeasurable and I will be forever grateful.

I'd also like to express my gratitude to the CEOs, entrepreneurs, and entertainers who so kindly gave of their time and wisdom to this project. And of course, I couldn't have done it without all the readers and listeners of Modern Manners Guy around the world whose e-mails, Facebook posts, and tweets gave me tons of fodder for this book. You have no idea how amazing it is that you trust me with your stories. It's always such a relief to know that I'm not the only one who feels like going mad when coworkers, friends, or family make manners faux pas. Your tales make this job a blast.

Last, but certainly not least, I'd like to thank the love of my life, my wife Jamie, and my two beautiful children, Maddy and Cole. Whether it's being woken up by me pacing the living room at 3:00 A.M. to knock out another chapter, turning off the side of the road to write down an idea, or skipping out to a coffee shop for hours to work, it would not have been possible without their love, support, and tireless patience. I thank you for being my greatest fans.